JESSICA
JONES

ALIAS INVESTIGATIONS

NEW YORK, NY

JESSICA JONES WAS ONCE THE COSTUMED
SUPER HERO KNOWN AS JEWEL.
SHE SUCKED AT IT.

NOW SHE'S A PRIVATE INVESTIGATOR AT
HER OWN FIRM, ALIAS INVESTIGATIONS.
SHE SUCKS LESS AT THAT.

WITH THE PURPLE MAN GONE, HER RELATIONSHIP
WITH HER HUSBAND, LUKE CAGE, AND THEIR
DAUGHTER, DANIELLE, IS BETTER THAN EVER.

BUT THERE'S ALWAYS ANOTHER CASE.

JESSICA JONES: BLIND SPOT. First printing 2018. ISBN 978-1-302-91292-5. Published by MARVEL WORLDWIDE, INC., a subsidiary of MARVEL ENTERTAINMENT, LLC. OFFICE OF PUBLICATION: 135 West 50th Street, New York, NY 10020. **Printed in the U.S.A.** DAN BUCKLEY, President, Marvel Entertainment; JOHN NEE, Publisher; JOE QUESADA, Chief Creative Officer; TOM BREVOORT, SVP of Publishing; DAVID BOGART, SVP of Business Affairs & Operations, Publishing & Partnership; DAVID GABRIEL, SVP of Sales & Marketing, Publishing; JEFF YOUNGQUIST, VP of Production & Special Projects; DAN CARR, Executive Director of Publishing Technology; ALEX MORALES, Director of Publishing Operations; DAN EDINGTON, Managing Editor; SUSAN CRESPI, Production Manager; STAN LEE, Chairman Emeritus. For information regarding advertising in Marvel Comics or on Marvel.com, please contact Vit DeBellis, Custom Solutions & Integrated Advertising Manager, at vdebellis@marvel.com. For Marvel subscription inquiries, please call 888-511-5480. **Manufactured between 9/7/2018 and 10/9/2018 by LSC COMMUNICATIONS INC., KENDALLVILLE, IN, USA.**

10 9 8 7 6 5 4 3 2 1

JESSICA JONES

Blind Spot

Writer: **Kelly Thompson**
Artists: **Mattia De Iulis** (#1-5)
& **Marcio Takara** (#6)
Color Artists: **Mattia De Iulis** (#1-5)
& **Rachelle Rosenberg** (#6)

Letterer: **VC's Cory Petit**
Cover Art: **Martin Simmonds**

Assistant Editor: **Alanna Smith**
Editor: **Tom Brevoort**

Based on characters created by **Brian Michael Bendis** & **Michael Gaydos**

Collection Editor: **Jennifer Grünwald** • Assistant Editor: **Caitlin O'Connell**
Associate Managing Editor: **Kateri Woody** • Editor, Special Projects: **Mark D. Beazley**
VP Production & Special Projects: **Jeff Youngquist** • SVP Print, Sales & Marketing: **David Gabriel**
Book Designer: **Jay Bowen**

Editor in Chief: **C.B. Cebulski** • Chief Creative Officer: **Joe Quesada**
President: **Dan Buckley** • Executive Producer: **Alan Fine**

POLICE LINE DO NOT CROSS
POLICE LINE DO NOT CROSS
POLICE LINE DO
CONFIDENTIAL
POLICE
LINE
DO NOT CROSS
DO NOT CROSS

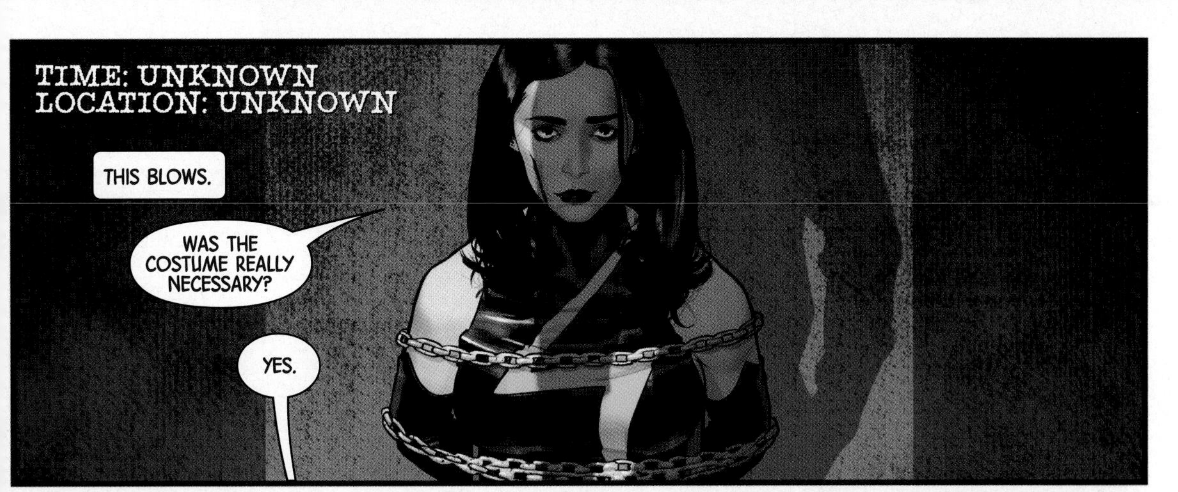
TIME: UNKNOWN
LOCATION: UNKNOWN
THIS BLOWS.
WAS THE COSTUME REALLY NECESSARY?
YES.

YOU COULDN'T AT LEAST GET ONE OF MINE? A JEWEL COSTUME? I MEAN, I WAS A SUPER HERO ONCE.
AS IF I COULD FIND A JEWEL COSTUME...THEY COULDN'T HAVE MADE MORE THAN A DOZEN OF THOSE.

OUCH.
I DON'T THINK YOU REALLY WANT TO DO THIS.
IT'S NOT A MATTER OF WHAT I WANT.
THEY ALWAYS SAY THAT.
THEY?

PEOPLE LIKE YOU. THE TERRIBLE THINGS THEY DO ARE SOMEHOW NEVER THEIR FAULT.
REMEMBER THAT WHEN I GET FREE.
WHAT I DO ISN'T GOING TO BE MY FAULT EITHER.

TIME: SATURDAY, 11:41 AM
LOCATION: HELL'S KITCHEN PARK
...AND THEN WHEN YOU'RE DONE AT THE BIRTHDAY PARTY, CAN YOU PLEASE PICK UP SOME MILK AND THAT CEREAL THAT SHE LIKES, THE ONE WITH THE LITTLE...
OOF.
LUKE, ARE YOU LISTENING?
YEAH, YEAH, SORRY. I'M LISTENING. KEEP GOING. BIRTHDAY PARTY. MILK. CEREAL WITH THE SHAPES.
RIGHT. AND ALSO A NEW LIGHT BULB FOR THE HALL--
THIS GUY GOES RIGHT EVERY TIME. I MEAN, HOW CAN THEY NOT SEE THIS?
LUKE!
I'M SORRY, BABY, BUT SERIOUSLY, THESE KIDS...MY MAN IN THE RED SHORTS CANNOT GO LEFT. HE SCORES EVERY TIME--
--BUT HE'S NOT THAT GOOD, HE'S GOT NO LEFT.
AND THESE KIDS, THEY'RE JUST NOT SEEING IT. IT'S UNBELIEVABLE.
UNBELIEVABLE? REALLY?
IT--IT'S PRETTY SERIOUS. WHAT HAPPENED TO GOOD FUNDAMENTALS IN THIS COUNTRY?
ARE WE TALKING ABOUT THE FUNDAMENTALS OF BASKETBALL?
WHAT OTHER FUNDAMENTALS ARE THERE?
FUN-DAMENTAL!

AND YOU CAN SAVE THEM FROM THIS LACK-OF-FUNDAMENTALS FATE?
I CAN.
YOU'VE GOT HALF AN HOUR BEFORE I HAVE TO BE AT THE OFFICE.
THAT'S MY GIRL.
YES, WELL, I'LL BE EXPECTING SOME KIND OF REWARD LATER.
CONSIDER IT DONE.
MY MEN! YOU'RE GOING ABOUT THIS ALL WRONG!
LUKE CAGE. NO WAY.
ARE YOU GONNA PLAY WITH US? REALLY?
YOU SEE THE SIZE OF HIS ARMS?
PRETTY HARD TO MISS.
I USED TO THINK IT WAS A BAD IDEA TO ENJOY A MOMENT LIKE THIS. LIKE I DIDN'T DESERVE IT.
AND LATER, I *KNEW* I DESERVED IT, BUT I WAS STILL CRIPPLED BY THE IDEA THAT RECOGNIZING THINGS BEING GOOD--ME BEING HAPPY--WAS A SURE WAY TO JINX IT ALL, MAKE IT DISAPPEAR.
LET'S TALK A LITTLE BIT ABOUT DEFENSE...

TIME:
SATURDAY, 12:22 PM
LOCATION:
ALIAS
INVESTIGATIONS
NOWADAYS I KNOW HOW IMPORTANT IT IS TO BASK IN THE GOOD, BECAUSE BAD WILL INEVITABLY FIND ME.
?!
LIKE I WAS SAYING, BAD FINDS ME.

SOMETIMES VERY, VERY BAD.
SHE'S ALREADY COLD. DEFINITELY DEAD. DAMMIT.
THANK GOD LUKE TOOK DANI.
HANDS IN THE AIR, NOW!
I'M GOING TO NEED MORE WORDS FOR "BAD."

MY NAME IS JESSICA JONES, I'M A P.I. THIS IS MY OFFICE. I WAS JUST CALLING 9-1-1--
DROP THE PHONE!
CAN I JUST... SET IT DOWN...IT'S BRAND NEW AND THESE SCREENS...
DROP IT!
ALL RIGHT, THEN.
I HEAR YOU GOT POWERS?
YES.
WELL, DON'T MOVE, DAMMIT.
I'M NOT MOVING.
CRACK
ALWAYS WITH THE KNEE IN THE BACK. EVERY COP I'VE EVER MET HAD A HARD-ON FOR THAT KNEE-IN-THE-BACK CRAP.
OOF.
UNG...
THIS WHOLE SITUATION HAS SETUP WRITTEN ALL OVER IT.

TIME: SATURDAY, 6:51 PM
LOCATION:
MIDTOWN NORTH
PRECINCT – "THE BOX"
NO PHONE CALL. NO INTERROGATION. SITTING HERE FOR HOURS. ALONE.
IF ONLY THEY KNEW THE RESTRAINT IT TAKES TO NOT BREAK THESE DAMN CUFFS IN HALF WHEN YOU HAVE AN ITCH YOU CAN'T REACH. OR MAYBE THEY *DO* KNOW.
THAT'S WHAT THEY'RE WAITING FOR, OF COURSE. FOR ME TO LOSE IT. THAT'S THEIR FAVORITE THING.
AND THESE TWO. REAL PRINCES LEAVING ME HERE FOR HOURS.
DETECTIVE CELLINO. THE "DISTINGUISHED" VETERAN. SAME OLD STORY: HE'S SEEN TOO MUCH.
DETECTIVE McGILL. YOUNG AND PRETENDING NOT TO BE.
OLD PIERCING SCAR
IMPRESSIVE 'STACHE.
DRY CLEANING OVERDUE.
SHAVING NICK.
NECK TATTOO
DONUTS OR COKE? DONUTS.
THE THING ABOUT BEING A P.I....IS THAT IT CHANGES HOW YOU SEE. IT WASN'T SOME SUPER-POWER I WAS BORN WITH, IT WAS JUST SOMETHING I LEARNED.
BUT ONCE YOU LEARN IT, THERE'S NO UNLEARNING IT. YOU CAN'T TURN IT OFF.
NOT A WEDDING BAND LINE...INTERESTING.
CHEWED FINGER NAILS.
AND THAT CAN BE A BURDEN.
BUT EVEN I HAVE BLIND SPOTS. AND BLIND SPOTS ALWAYS LEAD TO BAD SURPRISES. EVERY GODDAMN TIME.

MAKING ME WAIT THIS LONG CAN MEAN A COUPLE THINGS. ONE IS THAT THEY'RE GOING OVER MY OFFICE WITH A FINE-TOOTH COMB LOOKING FOR SOMETHING TO TIE ME TO THIS BODY.

I'VE BEEN HERE FOR SIX HOURS. I WANT MY GODDAMN PHONE CALL.
A.K.A. THEY'VE ACTUALLY GOT NOTHING.

SURE, SURE. JUST A COUPLE QUESTIONS.
YOU'VE GOT POWERS, RIGHT?

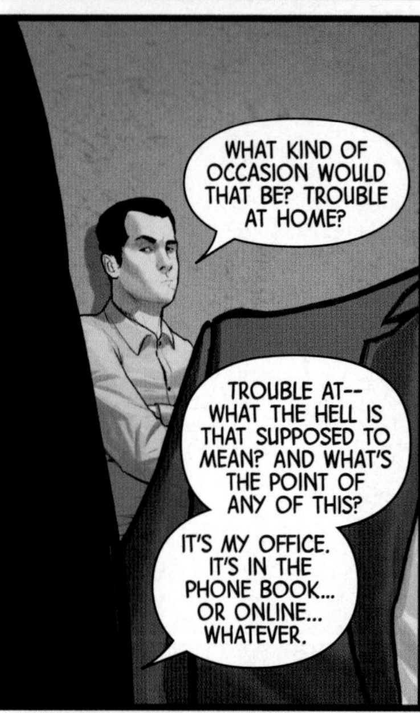
WHAT KIND OF OCCASION WOULD THAT BE? TROUBLE AT HOME?
TROUBLE AT-- WHAT THE HELL IS THAT SUPPOSED TO MEAN? AND WHAT'S THE POINT OF ANY OF THIS?
IT'S MY OFFICE. IT'S IN THE PHONE BOOK... OR ONLINE... WHATEVER.

SOMETIMES I WORK A LONG CASE AND CRASH OUT...WHAT DO YOU CARE? AND WHAT IS ALL OF THIS REALLY ABOUT?

INVESTIGATION
I NOTICE YOU HAVEN'T ASKED IF THE GIRL IS OKAY.

RIDICULOUS.
AND JUST HOW EXACTLY DID THAT HAPPEN, BY THE WAY? A WHOLE NYPD CONTINGENT DESCENDING ON ME LIKE SOME KIND OF BAD MOVIE?
WE GOT A TIP.
LEMME GUESS. ANONYMOUS.
YEAH, THAT'S NOT SUSPICIOUS AT ALL.

UNLESS YOU'RE CHARGING ME, YOU NEED TO LET ME GO.
YOU MIGHT NOT WANT TO MAKE THAT THREAT.

SO, YOU SAY YOU DON'T KNOW THIS GIRL?

YES. FOR THE TENTH TIME THAT I'VE BEEN ASKED THAT TODAY. YES.
WHAT KIND?
I DON'T REALLY SEE HOW THAT'S ANY OF YOUR BUSINESS.

WELL, THERE WAS A DEAD WOMAN IN YOUR APARTMENT, SO IT COULD BE RELEVANT--
IT'S NOT MY APARTMENT, IT'S MY *OFFICE.*
SO YOU *DON'T* LIVE THERE?

NO.
BECAUSE THERE'S A BED.
I SAID I DIDN'T LIVE THERE, I DIDN'T SAY I DON'T SLEEP THERE ON OCCASION.

WAIT. SHE'S ALIVE? THAT'S--
OH NO, SHE'S DEFINITELY DEAD. HOW DID YOU KNOW THAT?

HOW DID I...? ARE YOU KIDDING ME? SHE HAD NO PULSE. I WAS CHECKING IT WHEN YOUR PEOPLE BURST IN--

--CATCHING *YOU* RED-HANDED.

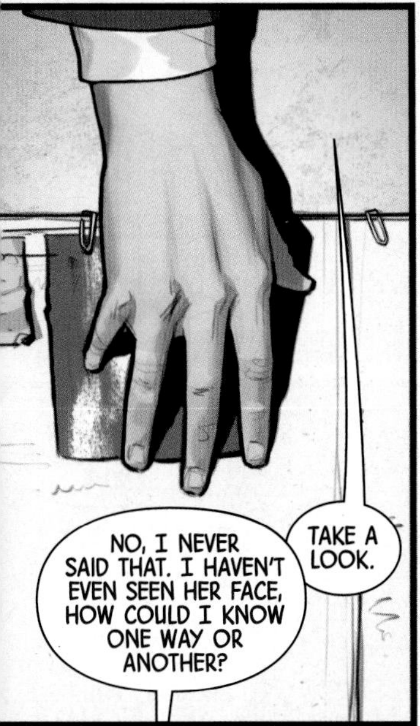
NO, I NEVER SAID THAT. I HAVEN'T EVEN SEEN HER FACE, HOW COULD I KNOW ONE WAY OR ANOTHER?
TAKE A LOOK.

WELL, SHIT. I *DO* KNOW HER.
THERE'S THAT BLIND SPOT.

IT'S DIA.
BINGO. THAT LOOKS LIKE RECOGNITION TO ME.

BLIND SPOT.
BAD SURPRISE.
I--I JUST DON'T KNOW WHAT TO DO ANYMORE, MS. JONES.
TIME: ABOUT SIX YEARS AGO
TAKE IT SLOW. JUST... TELL ME WHAT THE PROBLEM IS.
DIA SLOANE. AN OLD COLD CASE OF MINE. ONE THAT GOT AWAY...OR RATHER, ONE I FAILED TO SOLVE. AND NOW, MAYBE, ONE THAT'S COME BACK TO KILL HER.
BLUE-ISH HAIR.
HAUNTED EYES.
BRUISE ON HER NECK.
CHEAP CRYSTAL NECKLACE.
OBSCURE BAND T-SHIRT.
WHAT DID I MISS WITH DIA SLOANE THAT MIGHT HAVE LED TO HER DEATH?
I MEAN... THE PROBLEM IS *ME.*
HOW SO?
WELL, I...I MEAN, HAVE YOU EVER...HAVE YOU EVER JUST BEEN TOO WEAK? CAN YOU POSSIBLY KNOW WHAT THAT FEELS LIKE?
...
HER CASE ALWAYS HIT CLOSE TO THE BONE. IS THAT WHY I DIDN'T FOLLOW UP WHEN IT WENT BAD? IS THAT WHY I LET IT LINGER, UNSOLVED?
IS THAT WHY I DIDN'T CARE WHEN I FAILED HER SO SPECTACULARLY?
OF COURSE YOU DON'T. SO STUPID OF ME. YOU WERE, LIKE, AN AVENGER OR SOMETHING.
NO. I WASN'T AN AVENGER. NOT EVEN CLOSE. AND I...
WHAT'S WRONG?
NOTHING. WHAT IS IT THAT YOU THINK MAKES YOU WEAK? WHAT BROUGHT YOU HERE, ***SPECIFICALLY?***

RIGHT. OKAY. MY BOYFRIEND, JARED. I'VE BEEN IN LOVE WITH HIM FOR ALMOST AS LONG AS I CAN REMEMBER. SINCE HIGH SCHOOL.
BUT HE'S...I DON'T KNOW, HE'S DOING BAD THINGS.

HE HURTS YOU?
NO...YES. I MEAN, NOT PHYSICALLY, NO. AND NOT ALL THE TIME, BUT, YES, IT'S GOTTEN INCREASINGLY DIFFICULT BETWEEN US.
TO BE HONEST, DIA, THIS SOUNDS LIKE MAYBE IT'S A MATTER FOR THE POLICE. YOU MIGHT NEED PROTECTION.

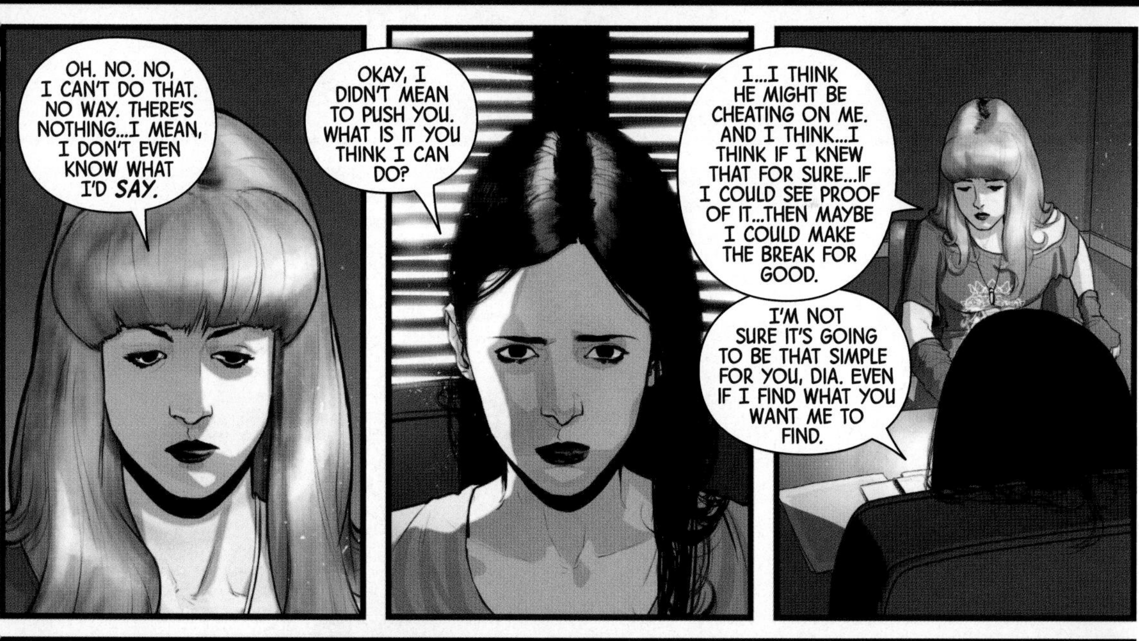
OH. NO. NO, I CAN'T DO THAT. NO WAY. THERE'S NOTHING...I MEAN, I DON'T EVEN KNOW WHAT I'D *SAY.*
OKAY, I DIDN'T MEAN TO PUSH YOU. WHAT IS IT YOU THINK I CAN DO?
I...I THINK HE MIGHT BE CHEATING ON ME. AND I THINK...I THINK IF I KNEW THAT FOR SURE...IF I COULD SEE PROOF OF IT...THEN MAYBE I COULD MAKE THE BREAK FOR GOOD.
I'M NOT SURE IT'S GOING TO BE THAT SIMPLE FOR YOU, DIA. EVEN IF I FIND WHAT YOU WANT ME TO FIND.

I...I KNOW. BUT I NEED TO AT LEAST TRY. I NEED TO KNOW THE TRUTH. AND MAYBE IT'LL SET ME FREE. MUST BE A SAYING FOR A REASON, RIGHT?

SO YOU DO KNOW HER.
DIA SLOANE. SHE WAS A CLIENT OF MINE A FEW YEARS BACK.
TIME: SATURDAY, 7:01 PM
LOCATION: MIDTOWN NORTH PRECINCT

WE'RE GONNA NEED MORE THAN THAT.
⇾SIGH⇽ I DON'T HAVE MUCH. I FOUND A CHEATING BOYFRIEND, TOOK A FEW PICTURES. BUT SHE DISAPPEARED.
I WENT LOOKING FOR HER BECAUSE THE BOYFRIEND SEEMED A BIT UNSTABLE. BUT I DIDN'T FIND HER.
SOME P.I.

AND HIS NAME?
I DON'T REMEMBER. I CAN CHECK MY FILES. BUT THERE WAS AN EXPLOSION A WHILE BACK. I LOST ALMOST EVERYTHING.
THAT'S NOT GOOD ENOUGH, JONES.

IT'LL HAVE TO BE.
LET'S GO, JESSICA.
YEAH?
ABSOLUTELY. CHARGE HER OR UNCUFF HER, DETECTIVES.
MURDOCK, YOU CAN'T JUST--
YOU KNOW VERY WELL I CAN. THIS IS MY CLIENT, AND YOU GUYS HAVE GOT NOTHING TO HOLD HER ON. YOU DON'T EVEN HAVE A CAUSE OF DEATH.
IF YOU FIND SOME ACTUAL EVIDENCE TYING MY CLIENT TO THE BODY, FEEL FREE TO GIVE US A CALL AND WE'LL COME BACK IN.
BUT FOR NOW...SHE'S BEEN EXCEEDINGLY PATIENT GIVEN THE CIRCUMSTANCES. LET US LEAVE BEFORE I HAVE TO SUE YOU. I HATE THE PAPERWORK.
THANK CHRIST.
SNAP
LATER, BOYS.

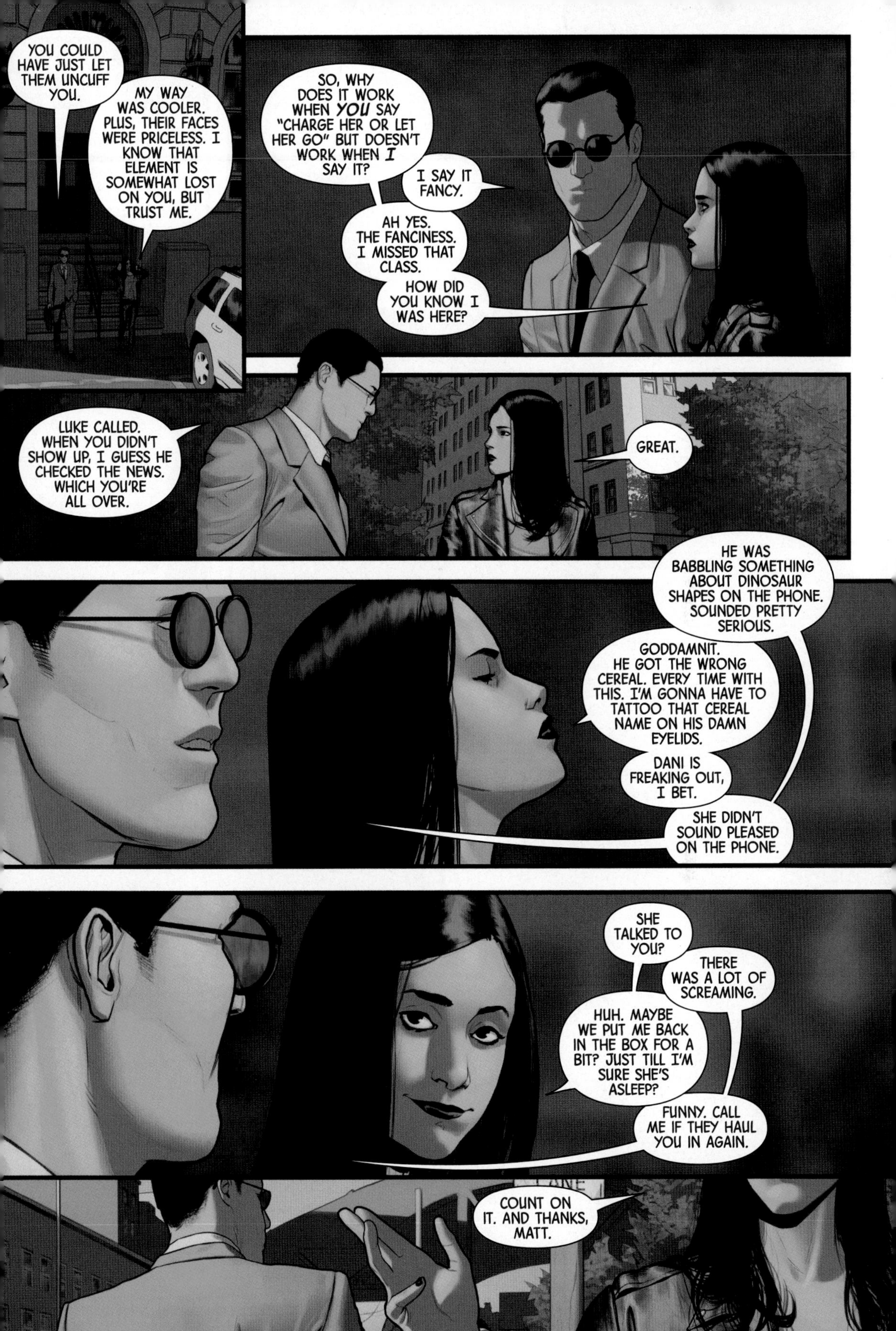
YOU COULD HAVE JUST LET THEM UNCUFF YOU.
MY WAY WAS COOLER. PLUS, THEIR FACES WERE PRICELESS. I KNOW THAT ELEMENT IS SOMEWHAT LOST ON YOU, BUT TRUST ME.
SO, WHY DOES IT WORK WHEN *YOU* SAY "CHARGE HER OR LET HER GO" BUT DOESN'T WORK WHEN *I* SAY IT?
I SAY IT FANCY.
AH YES. THE FANCINESS. I MISSED THAT CLASS.
HOW DID YOU KNOW I WAS HERE?
LUKE CALLED. WHEN YOU DIDN'T SHOW UP, I GUESS HE CHECKED THE NEWS. WHICH YOU'RE ALL OVER.
GREAT.
HE WAS BABBLING SOMETHING ABOUT DINOSAUR SHAPES ON THE PHONE. SOUNDED PRETTY SERIOUS.
GODDAMNIT. HE GOT THE WRONG CEREAL. EVERY TIME WITH THIS. I'M GONNA HAVE TO TATTOO THAT CEREAL NAME ON HIS DAMN EYELIDS.
DANI IS FREAKING OUT, I BET.
SHE DIDN'T SOUND PLEASED ON THE PHONE.
SHE TALKED TO YOU?
THERE WAS A LOT OF SCREAMING.
HUH. MAYBE WE PUT ME BACK IN THE BOX FOR A BIT? JUST TILL I'M SURE SHE'S ASLEEP?
FUNNY. CALL ME IF THEY HAUL YOU IN AGAIN.
COUNT ON IT. AND THANKS, MATT.
YOU'RE WELCOME.

TIME: SATURDAY, 8:09 PM LOCATION: ALIAS INVESTIGATIONS
--WELL, I'LL PICK UP THE RIGHT CEREAL WHEN I COME HOME, LUKE.
YOU'RE NOT COMING NOW?
YOU'VE GOT TO BE KIDDING ME. MATT DIDN'T SAY IT WOULD STILL BE SEALED.
I'VE GOT TO DO SOME WORK AT THE OFFICE...CALL THE CLIENT FOR THE APPOINTMENT I MISSED THIS AFTERNOON, SEE IF ANY OF DIA SLOANE'S CASE FILES SURVIVED THE EXPLOSION. BUT I'LL BE QUICK. I PROMISE.
I'VE HEARD THAT BEFORE. →SIGH← ALL RIGHT. TRY TO HURRY. I'LL ORDER CHINESE FROM THE GOOD PLACE IN AN HOUR. LET THAT BE YOUR MOTIVATION IF NOTHING ELSE.
WELL PLAYED. YOU KNOW ME TOO WELL, MR. CAGE.
I LOVE YOU. BUT I WILL NOT SAVE YOU ANY SOUP DUMPLINGS IF YOU'RE LATE.
KSSHH
FAIR.
I LOVE YOU, TOO. KISS DANI FOR ME.
JUST GREAT.
ENOUGH FINGERPRINT DUST IN HERE TO KILL A MAN.

YOU KNOW WHAT TAKES A HIT WHEN YOUR OFFICE EXPLODES THANKS TO GODDAMN MARIA HILL? YOUR OLD CASE FILES.
I KNOW I SHOULD GO DIGITAL, BUT THEN THEY WANT YOU TO USE THAT CLOUD THING, AND WHAT IS THAT CLOUD BUT SOMEONE ELSE'S SERVER?

WHY WOULD I KEEP *MY* STUFF ON SOMEONE *ELSE'S* SERVER? DOESN'T *SOUND* SECURE, THAT'S FOR DAMN SURE.
SLOANE, D.
STILL. I BET CLOUDS BLOW UP IN BIG S.H.I.E.L.D.-RELATED EXPLOSIONS LESS THAN MY OFFICE DOES.

DIA SLOANE WAS THE RARE CLIENT WHO ACTUALLY *DID* WANT ME TO DISCOVER HER BOYFRIEND WAS THE DIRTBAG SHE SUSPECTED HE WAS. SHE THOUGHT SHE NEEDED SOMETHING TO PUSH HER OVER THE EDGE. SHE THOUGHT THAT WOULD BE IT.
I DOUBTED THAT WOULD MAKE A DIFFERENCE...BUT I NEVER GOT THE CHANCE TO FIND OUT.
I FAILED HER. AND IT COULD VERY WELL BE WHY SHE'S DEAD TODAY. I CAN'T BRING HER BACK, AND I'LL JUST...I'LL HAVE TO LIVE WITH THAT GUILT.
BUT I'M NOT ABOUT TO FAIL HER AGAIN. SHE CAME BACK TO MY OFFICE FOR A REASON, AND I'M NOT GOING TO STOP DIGGING UNTIL I FIND OUT WHAT HAPPENED TO HER AND WHY.
IF I CAN'T BRING HER PEACE, I CAN AT LEAST BRING HER JUSTICE.

TIME: SATURDAY, 11:59 PM
LOCATION: ALIAS INVESTIGATIONS
...
12:01
Luke Cage
Missed calls (3)
DAMMIT.

JUST WAKE UP THE REST OF THE WAY AND WALK HOME, JONES--
TMP

...
LUKE, MAYBE?
NO. NOT LUKE. LUKE IS LOUDER THAN THIS.
HE ALSO DOESN'T MAKE THE HAIRS ON MY ARM STAND ON END.

NERVES SO TIGHT I FEEL LIKE MY TENDONS ARE GOING TO SNAP.
CAN'T REMEMBER IF I LEFT THAT WINDOW OPEN.
...
KSSSH

HEART HAMMERING SO HARD I CAN'T HEAR MYSELF THINK.
I FEEL SO STRANGE...WEAK... POWERLESS.
SOMETHING'S *WRONG.*
DON'T--
BLAM

NOT SO POWERFUL NOW, ARE YA?

2

TIME: UNKNOWN
LOCATION: UNKNOWN
IS THAT SUPPOSED TO BE A THREAT?
THIS IS THE PART WHERE I'M SUPPOSED TO SAY, "NO, IT'S A PROMISE."
OH, IT'S 100% A THREAT.

KRRRK
ANY CHANCE I COULD GET A MASSEUSE IN HERE? MY NECK IS REALLY CRAMPING UP.
HEH. I'LL LOOK INTO IT.

COOL. ANY CHANCE WE CAN CHANGE CHEFS?
I HAVEN'T FED YOU ANYTHING.
YES. THIS IS MY POINT. CLEARLY WE NEED A NEW CHEF.

YOU THINK YOU'RE VERY FUNNY, DON'T YOU?
EH. I'M ALL RIGHT.
SHE THOUGHT SHE WAS FUNNY, TOO. AND LOOK WHAT HAPPENED TO HER.

TIME: SUNDAY, 3:18 PM
LOCATION: MOUNT SINAI HOSPITAL

YOU ATE ALL THE SOUP DUMPLINGS ALREADY, DIDN'T YOU?

YOU'RE GODDAMN RIGHT I DID, JESS. YOU SAID YOU'D BE HOME IN AN HOUR--
OH BOY. HE'S A MESS. I GOTTA DOWNPLAY THIS BEING-SHOT-IN-THE-HEAD BUSINESS.
--THIS WAS WAAAAAY MORE THAN AN HOUR.
FAIR.
BUT WHAT *DID* HAPPEN? HOW AM I ALIVE?
I FELT IT, IT WAS BRUTAL. AND IT WAS *OVER.* THE BIG LACK OF SHINING LIGHT AND EVERYTHING.
BABY, I REALLY THOUGHT I LOST YOU.
I KNOW... BUT I'M OKAY.
SOMEHOW.
LUKE, YOU'RE CRUSHING ME.
I KNOW.
BABE, I KNOW I'M USUALLY INTO IT BUT MAYBE NOT RIGHT NOW, HUH?
SHHHH.

WHERE'S DANI? AND PLEASE TELL ME THERE AREN'T, LIKE, A BILLION SUPER HERO TYPES IN THE LOBBY.
UM...

AH, GEEZ. I'M GONNA HAVE TO MURDER LUKE NOW. CALLING EVERYONE WE KNOW JUST FOR A RUN-OF-THE-MILL BULLET TO THE BRAIN.
WELL, OKAY, WHEN YOU PUT ALL THE WORDS IN A SENTENCE TOGETHER LIKE THAT, IT DOES SEEM LIKE MAYBE IT'S THE TIME TO ACTUALLY CALL IN ALL THE FAMILY. I'LL FORGIVE HIM...
NOT THE LOBBY, JONES.
...BUT NOT FOR EATING THE LAST SOUP DUMPLING. THAT'S A DIVORCE-LEVEL OFFENSE RIGHT THERE.
Happy Birthday
MOMMA!
THERE'S ALSO THE PESKY QUESTION OF WHO THE HELL SHOT ME. AND HOW I'M NOT STILL DEAD.
HI, BABY.

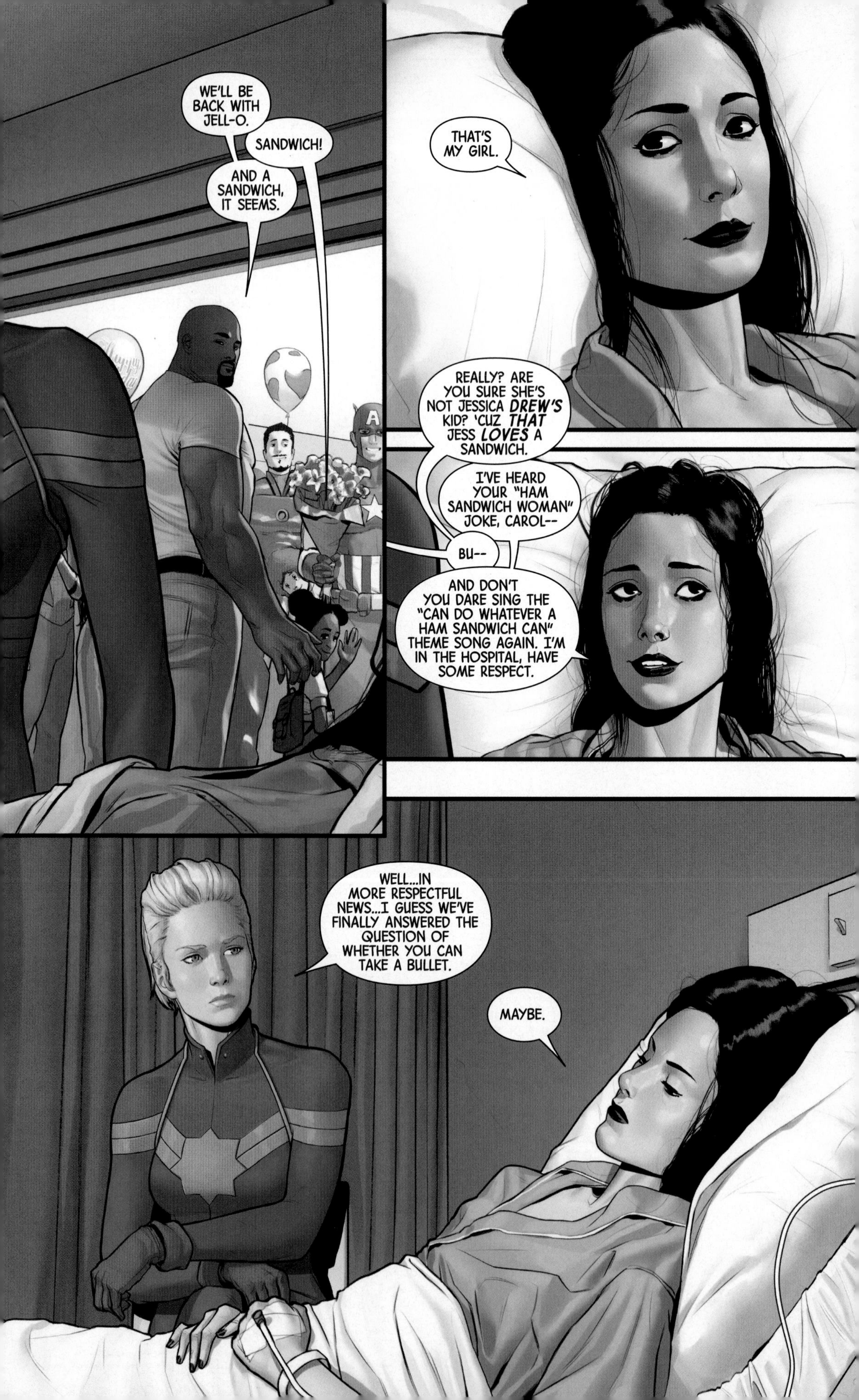
WE'LL BE BACK WITH JELL-O.
SANDWICH!
AND A SANDWICH, IT SEEMS.
THAT'S MY GIRL.
REALLY? ARE YOU SURE SHE'S NOT JESSICA DREW'S KID? 'CUZ THAT JESS LOVES A SANDWICH.
I'VE HEARD YOUR "HAM SANDWICH WOMAN" JOKE, CAROL--
BU--
AND DON'T YOU DARE SING THE "CAN DO WHATEVER A HAM SANDWICH CAN" THEME SONG AGAIN. I'M IN THE HOSPITAL, HAVE SOME RESPECT.
WELL...IN MORE RESPECTFUL NEWS...I GUESS WE'VE FINALLY ANSWERED THE QUESTION OF WHETHER YOU CAN TAKE A BULLET.
MAYBE.

MAYBE? YOU'RE SITTING HERE, AREN'T YOU?
I AM, BUT I DID GET SHOT IN THE HEAD. I MEAN, I'M NOT TRYING TO HARP ON IT BECAUSE I DON'T WANT TO FREAK LUKE OUT ANY MORE THAN HE ALREADY IS... BUT I WAS DEAD. I KNOW IT.
YOU--
WAS DEAD. SURE OF IT.
BUT THAT'S NOT WHAT THE EMTs AND DOCTORS SAY. THEY FOUND A BULLET BUT NO WOUND.
I'M TELLING YOU. YOU KNOW WHEN YOU'RE DEAD.
ALL RIGHT, ALL RIGHT. DON'T TALK TO ME LIKE I'VE NEVER BEEN DEAD BEFORE.
SOMETHING WEIRD AS HELL IS GOING ON HERE. AND SINCE YOU'RE THE SUPER-FANCY CAPTAIN MARVEL...I NEED A FAVOR.
I'M GONNA ASK SOMEONE TO TAKE THE "SUPER-FANCY" OFF MY NAME...EVERYONE IS ALWAYS ASKING ME FOR FAVORS.
I DID YOU A PRETTY BIG FAVOR RECENTLY, AS I RECALL.
DAMN RIGHT IT DID.
GEEZ, OKAY. THAT BULLET TO THE BRAIN MADE YOU VERY DEMANDING.
I NEED THE BULLET.
I THINK THE NYPD IS GONNA WANT TO HOLD ON TO THAT.
YES, THAT'S WHERE THE FAVOR AND THE "YOU THROWING AROUND YOUR CAPTAIN MARVEL WEIGHT" THING COMES IN.
OKAY. I MEAN...I'LL TRY. BUT WHY?
JUST A P.I. HUNCH.
OH. MYSTERIOUS.
I KNOW.

TIME:
MONDAY, 8:43 AM
LOCATION:
MOUNT SINAI HOSPITAL
MS. JONES. YOU WERE SHOT IN THE HEAD...WE THINK. YOU CANNOT CHECK YOURSELF OUT IN UNDER 48 HOURS.
CANNOT. REALLY?
IT WOULD BE AGAINST MEDICAL ADVICE, YES. YOU'D HAVE TO SIGN A WAIVER.
NO PROBLEM.
BUT...
BUT WHAT? I'VE GOT SUPER-POWERS...I DON'T THINK WE CAN TREAT THIS LIKE I'M A NORMAL BULLET WOUND VICTIM.
I AGREE. BUT IT'S STILL WAY TOO SOON FOR YOU TO JUST WALK OUT OF HERE.
I FEEL FINE, DOC.
BUT WE STILL DON'T REALLY KNOW WHAT HAPPENED.

EXACTLY, AND WE'RE NOT GOING TO FIGURE IT OUT WITH ME STUCK IN HERE.

I GOTTA MOVE SOMEWHERE WHERE THERE'S NO SUPER HEROES.

HOW MANY TIMES I SAVE THIS CITY STILL CAN'T GET A CAB TO STOP DRIVES ME CRAZY--
LUKE. YOU'RE MUTTERING AGAIN.
I KNOW, IT CALMS ME DOWN.
SO HERE'S THE THING, BABE--
NO, NO, NO, NO. NO WAY, JESS. YOU'RE COMING HOME WITH ME.
EXCEPT SOMEONE KILLED ME, BABE. AND NOT ONLY DO I HAVE TO FIND THEM, BUT IF THEY COME BACK, I DON'T WANT THEM ANYWHERE NEAR YOU AND DANI.
SO WE GET A SITTER AND I STAY WITH YOU--
--AND WHAT IF WHOEVER CAME FOR ME COMES FOR DANI, LUKE? YOU ACTUALLY ARE BULLET-PROOF. WE NEED YOU WITH HER.
JESS...I CAN'T GO THROUGH THAT AGAIN.
BUT WE WILL. THIS IS OUR LIFE. DANGEROUS. ALWAYS HAS BEEN, ALWAYS WILL BE.
BUT I'M HARD TO KILL. AND I'LL DO ANYTHING TO COME BACK TO YOU. LET ME FIGURE THIS OUT.
YOU COME BACK TO ME OR ELSE, JONES.
I PROMISE.
HONK HONK
YO, YOU GETTING IN OR WHAT, MAN?!
REALLY?!
UH. I MEAN...TAKE YOUR TIME, OF COURSE.

TIME: MONDAY, 9:51 AM
LOCATION: THE SANCTUM SANCTORUM, HOME OF DOCTOR STRANGE
BANG
BANG
BANG
STRANGE! STRAAAAAANGE!
JESSICA JONES. IT IS EXTREMELY EARLY.
IT'S ALMOST TEN.
I STAND BY MY STATEMENT.
IS THERE ANY CHANCE I CAN PERSUADE YOU TO GO AWAY?
NO.
I THOUGHT NOT.
VERY WELL. DO COME IN, THEN.
OOOH. ROUGH NIGHT? WE CAN HELP, GIRL.
WE ARE EXTRA HELPFUL, LADY.
AND WE'RE REFORMED. SO NICE. SO HELPFUL.
UH.
I WOULD TELL YOU NOT TO TALK TO THE SNAKES, BUT I SLIGHTLY HOPE THEY DEVOUR YOU, SO DO WHAT YOU WANT.
GEE. THANKS.
THEY NEVER STOP. WHY DO THEY NEVER STOP?
I DON'T KNOW, BUT IT'S HORRIBLE.
IT'S STARTING TO AFFECT MY SELF-ESTEEM.
SELF-ESTEEM? THAT'S SOME KIND OF HUMAN BREAKFAST MEAT, RIGHT?

SO WHAT BRINGS YOU HERE AT THIS UNGODLY HOUR, JESSICA?
AGAIN, IT'S TEN A.M., BUT WHATEVER. I'M HERE ABOUT THIS.
A MAGIC BULLET?
IS IT?
IS IT A *BULLET?*
NO. *MAGIC.*
MAGIC, LIKE... IT MAKES RIGHT TURNS IN MIDAIR TO KILL PRESIDENTS... OR GOES IN YOUR BRAIN AND DOESN'T ACTUALLY KILL YOU?
SOMETHING? ANYTHING?
NO. IT'S JUST A REGULAR BULLET.
THEN WHY DID YOU CALL IT MAGIC?
I DID NOT THINK YOU WOULD BRING ME A *NORMAL* BULLET. WHAT A RIDICULOUS WASTE OF TIME *THAT* WOULD BE.
SO THERE'S NOTHING ODD ABOUT IT?
NO. BUT *YOU,* JONES...

...THERE'S DEFINITELY SOMETHING GOING ON WITH YOU.
NOT MAGIC, EXACTLY. BUT YOU'VE BEEN TOUCHED BY SOMETHING RECENTLY. IT'S ALL OVER YOU.
JUST GREAT.
GOOD LUCK, JONES. NEXT TIME, DON'T KNOCK UNTIL AFTER NOON UNLESS IT'S LIFE OR DEATH.
SLAM
DICK.

TIME: MONDAY, 3:01 PM
LOCATION: ALIAS INVESTIGATIONS
SO STRANGE WAS MOSTLY A STRIKEOUT.
BETTER GO INTO THE FILES AND USE THE TIME-HONORED P.I. TRICK OF DIGGING UNTIL YOU GO HALF BLIND.
BAND LOGO WITH SKULL MICKEL
OR AS THE CASE MAY BE HERE... FULLY BLIND.
PEOPLE REALLY LOVE THEIR CATS. CAN'T STOP THEMSELVES FROM TALKING ABOUT THEM. THAT'S DEFINITELY A THING.
DIA'S CAT WAS CALLED SOMETHING WEIRD. SOMETHING ABOUT MEAT. MR. MEAT? MEATHEAD? MEATBALL. THAT WAS IT.
OVER 600,000 RESULTS. GREAT.
Jessica Jones
#MEATBALL
#meatball

CLICK
CLICK
CLICK
CLICK
JESUS. HOW CAN THIS MANY PEOPLE WANT TO PHOTOGRAPH MEATBALLS? WHAT ARE PEOPLE DOING WITH THEIR TIME? IT'S--

WAIT. HERE WE GO. WHAT DOES THAT COLLAR SAY...76-3498... MAYBE?
PARTIAL PHONE NUMBER. IT'S A START. THAT PLUS THE SUPER-OBSCURE BAND T-SHIRT... MIGHT BE ENOUGH...
STOP HOVERING. COME IN OR GET OUT. I'M NOT TOO KEEN ON LOOMING SHADOWY FIGURES THESE DAYS.
REALLY, JONES?
DAMN RIGHT.
MISTY KNIGHT. NOT A FAN OF YOURS TRULY.
BEST HAIR IN TOWN.
WHY IS EVERY OFFICE YOU EVER HAVE SHIT, JONES?
DISAGREEABLE EXPRESSION.
CYBERNETIC ARM.
SHOULDER HOLSTER.
HEY, MISTY. ALTHOUGH JUDGING FROM THE STANDARD-ISSUE POLYESTER SUIT, I'M GUESSING IT'S "AGENT KNIGHT" OF SOME KIND?
FBI.
LET'S SEE THE BADGE.
POLYESTER JACKET.
A.C.D.? LOOKS LIKE YOU'RE MISSING A FINAL "C" THERE. ALSO, IF YOU'RE GOING FOR AC/DC YOU'RE GOING TO NEED TO LOOSEN WAY THE HELL UP.
AC/DC JOKES? I FEEL LIKE YOU'RE DATING YOURSELF, JONES.

SO WHAT'S IT STAND FOR? NO, WAIT, LET ME GUESS...
...ABNORMAL CRIME DIVISION?
ABERRANT CRIME DIVISION.
ABERRANT. YEAH, THAT'S NOT *TOO* OFFENSIVE.
WELL, I DIDN'T NAME IT.
SO YOU'RE BACK TO WORKING FOR THE MAN, HUH?
SOMETHING AND SOMEONE WAS GOING TO FILL THE VACUUM LEFT IN A WORLD WITHOUT S.H.I.E.L.D....I WASN'T WILLING TO TAKE A RISK ON *WHO* FILLED IT.
AND THIS NEW ABERRANT CRIME DIVISION IS YOUR ANSWER TO THAT POWER VACUUM?
IT'S AN ANSWER FOR NOW. I'M TAKING IT DAY BY DAY.
FAIR ENOUGH. SO YOU'RE HERE TO WHAT...TELL ME TO STOP MY INVESTIGATION?
OBVIOUSLY.
BUT YOU KNOW I'M NOT, GOING TO DO THAT.
OBVIOUSLY.
HOW ABOUT WE SKIP RIGHT TO THE PART WHERE WE AGREE TO SHARE INFORMATION IN THE BEST INTEREST OF EVERYONE.
...FINE.

YOU FIRST, JONES.
...ALL RIGHT. MY CLIENT WAS DIA SLOANE. THE EX-BOYFRIEND'S NAME WAS JARED BEEKMAN.
HERE'S LAST KNOWN ADDRESS FOR BOTH, THOUGH I DON'T THINK THEY'LL GET YOU FAR. SHE DISAPPEARED BEFORE I SOLVED HER CASE AND I NEVER FOUND HER.
WELL, YOU'RE A GREAT DETECTIVE.
SURE. YOUR TURN.
...
DON'T EVEN TRY IT, MISTY.
YOU'RE NOT THE FIRST WOMAN WITH POWERS TO GET SHOT IN THE HEAD IN THE LAST WEEK.
HOLY SHIT.
PLAY IT COOL. PRETEND YOU KNOW.
NO KIDDING. TELL ME SOMETHING I DON'T KNOW, KNIGHT.
YOU ***ARE*** THE FIRST ONE TO SURVIVE IT. WHITE RABBIT AND SKEIN APPEAR TO BE PERMANENTLY DEAD.
CRIME SCENE IS EERILY SIMILAR TO YOURS. PLUS, THEY'RE A COUPLE OF FEMALE D-LISTERS THAT EITHER HAD POWERS OR WERE PERCEIVED TO HAVE POWERS.
I'M NOT D-LIST.
JUST BARELY, THOUGH.
PFFT. COME ON.

PING
PING

NEWS
INFAMOUS MONSTER HUNTER & SUPER HERO
ELSA BLOODSTONE FOUND DEAD
SHIT.

WONDER WHERE ELSA'S BEEN CRASHING.
THERE ARE A COUPLE WAYS TO FIND OUT. THEY'VE ALL GOT DOWNSIDES. SOME MORE THAN OTHERS...

RINGRING
...BUT I'M SURE I CAN GET ELSA'S LATEST ADDRESS FROM NICO MINORU. I DON'T HAVE NICO'S NUMBER, BUT ALL THESE SUPER-KIDS KNOW EACH OTHER.
KATE'S A GOOD START. IF I CAN STOP HER FROM TALKING MY EAR OFF.
RINGRIN--

OHMIGOD! JESS! YOU'RE ACTUALLY CALLING ME! IHAVESOMUCH TOTELLYOU--
KATE BISHOP.

KATE. KATE. KATE.
WHAT?
THERE'S SOME URGENCY HERE, BISHOP. I NEED NICO MINORU'S NUMBER. I PROMISE I'LL CALL BACK FOR A CATCH-UP LATER. OKAY?
NO I WON'T.

OH. OKAY. SURE. YEAH, I DON'T ACTUALLY HAVE NICO'S NEW NUMBER, BUT I HAVE KAROLINA'S, AND I BET SHE CAN HELP.
PERFECT.

KAROLINA DEAN.
--OF COURSE I HAVE NICO'S NUMBER, BUT I DON'T GIVE IT OUT TO JUST ANYONE.
IT'S ABOUT ELSA BLOODSTONE.

OH! OH. I SAW THE NEWS. OKAY, HOLD ON.
THANKS.

NICO MINORU.
--LAST ADDRESS I HAVE IS A CONDO IN MIDTOWN, YOU HAVE A PEN?
...IS SHE...IS SHE OKAY?
I HONESTLY DON'T KNOW, NICO.

...OKAY.
I DIDN'T REALIZE THEY WERE SO CLOSE. MAYBE I SHOULD HAVE USED A LIGHTER TOUCH.

ONDAY, 8:39 PM
ON:
VN MANHATTAN,
OWN ADDRESS
BLOODSTONE
THREE CALLS. MINIMUM DRAMA. NOT BAD. THANK GOD I WAS ABLE TO AVOID THE X-MEN PHONE TREE...THAT THING IS A NIGHTMARE.
INTO
IME
IS
A BIT
HABIT.
AND THE DEJA VU EFFECT IS INTENSE. LET'S HOPE THIS TIME IT DOESN'T END WITH ME DEAD IN A POOL OF BLOOD.
...
WAIT--

YEAH, SO THAT HURT LIKE A SONOFABITCH.

WELL. ELSA BLOODSTONE. ALIVE AND WELL. THAT'S GOOD...MAYBE?
DON'T TELL ME YOU'RE BLOODY IN ON THIS, TOO, JONES.

3
CRIME SCENE - DO NOT CROSS
T.N.T.

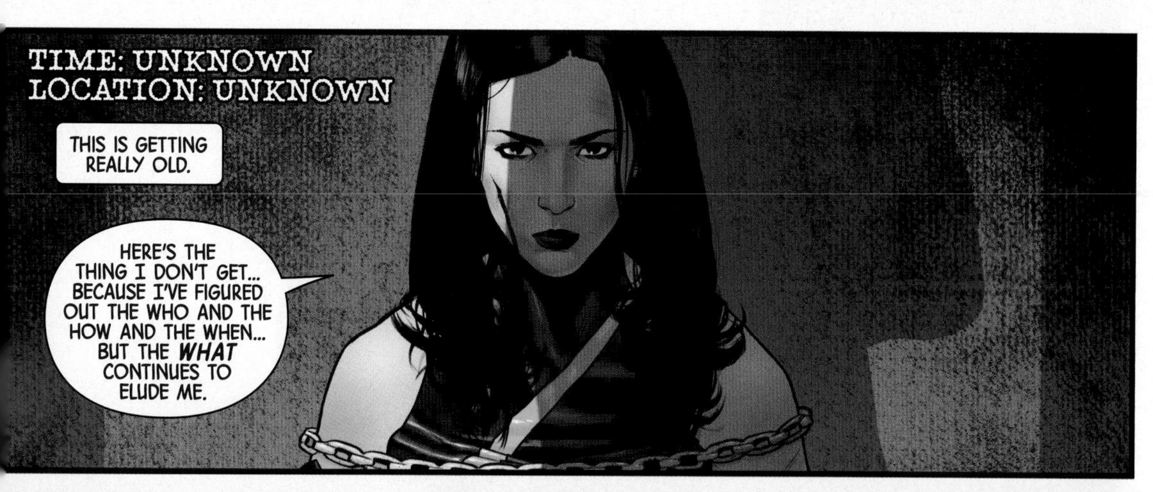
TIME: UNKNOWN
LOCATION: UNKNOWN
THIS IS GETTING REALLY OLD.
HERE'S THE THING I DON'T GET... BECAUSE I'VE FIGURED OUT THE WHO AND THE HOW AND THE WHEN... BUT THE WHAT CONTINUES TO ELUDE ME.

LIKE WHAT ARE YOU ACTUALLY GETTING OUT OF ANY OF THIS?
YOU'D NEVER UNDERSTAND.

TRY ME. I'M AN UNDERSTANDING PERSON WHO'S MADE MORE MISTAKES THAN ANY TEN PEOPLE SHOULD BE ALLOWED. WHAT'S THE HARM IN TRYING?
THE HARM? THE HARM IS YOU'RE TRYING TO TRICK ME. I HAVE A LONG LIST AND A SCHEDULE TO KEEP AND YOU KNOW THAT. YOU'RE JUST TRYING TO SLOW ME DOWN.

WELP. I HAD TO TRY. UNLIKE YOU, WHO CLEARLY HATES TO TRY. IT'S A MIRACLE YOU'VE EVER MANAGED TO GET ANYTHING DONE.
KEEP TALKING. YOU'RE ONLY MAKING IT WORSE FOR YOURSELF.
I MEAN... DOES IT GET WORSE THAN THIS?
YOU HAVE NO IDEA, BUT I PROMISE YOU YOU'RE GOING TO FIND OUT.

TIME: MONDAY, 8:41 PM
LOCATION: MIDTOWN MANHATTAN,
LAST KNOWN ADDRESS OF ELSA BLOODSTONE
ELSA BLOODSTONE. MONSTER HUNTER EXTRAORDINAIRE. MOUTH OF A SAILOR (AN EVEN DIRTIER SAILOR THAN ME).
HEARD SHE KILLED A MONSTER WITH A SPOON BEFORE SHE COULD WALK.
SOUNDS RIGHT.
INJURY.
HAIR TO RIVAL MISTY'S.
PISSED EXPRESSION.
SO, YOU BLOODY IN ON THIS OR WHAT, JONES?
BLOOD?
HOSPITAL I.D.
IT WOULD BE A REAL SHAME TO HAVE SURVIVED A BULLET TO THE HEAD TWO DAYS AGO ONLY TO HAVE ELSA BEAT ME TO A PULP IN HER LIVING ROOM.
LET'S SEE IF WE CAN AVOID THAT...
I AM ABOUT AS FAR FROM "IN ON THIS" AS POSSIBLE, ELSA.
I GOT SHOT TOO, TWO DAYS AGO... AND LIKE YOU, I'M MIRACULOUSLY FINE.

WELL. AREN'T WE A COUPLE OF BADASS MOTHER- BITCHES.
HEH.
EXCEPT... I DON'T THINK THAT'S IT AT ALL, DO YOU?
NO.
**** NO IS RIGHT. MY KIND OF ANSWER.

SO, MAYBE TOGETHER WE CAN FIGURE THIS OUT?
FINE BY ME, JONES, BUT WE'LL HAVE TO DO IT WHILE I WORK.
SURE. WHAT KIND OF--

--WORK?
JESUS. WELL, I SUPPOSE YOU HAVE TO USE MORE THAN HARSH LANGUAGE TO KILL MONSTERS.
OKAY, WELL, COULD WE JUST SIT DOWN FOR A SECOND *BEFORE* YOU GO? OR MAYBE GRAB A COFFEE OR SOMETHING?
DOES WHAT I'M PUTTING IN THIS BAG LOOK UNSERIOUS TO YOU, DARLING? DOES IT LOOK LIKE IT CAN BLOODY WAIT?
NO. YOU'RE RIGHT...IT LOOKS ON THE, UH, URGENT SIDE.
DAMN RIGHT. I WAS PACKING WEAPONS SO I COULD HEAD OFF MONSTERS IN THE HUDSON RIVER WHEN I GOT SHOT IN THE BACK OF THE BLOODY ☠☠☠☠ HEAD.
NO, INSTEAD I IMAGINE THAT, AFTER I GOT TAKEN OUT, EVERYTHING GOT WAY ☠☠☠☠ WORSE. SO YOU CAN INTERVIEW ME WHILE I BASH IN MONSTER HEADS, OR YOU CAN WAIT IN LINE.
AND IT'S NOT LIKE THOSE MONSTERS JUST WENT, *"OH, GREAT, LET'S GIVE UP ON TRYING TO EAT PEOPLE!"*
WELL, OKAY THEN.
WHEN YOU SAY IN THE HUDSON RIVER, YOU DON'T MEAN LITERALLY *IN* THE HUDSON RIVER, RIGHT?
HELL YES, I DO.
WELL, CRAP.

LOCATION: SHORE OF THE HUDSON RIVER
SECOND I STILL THOUGHT YOU MIGHT BE JOKING ABOUT IT BEING *IN* THE HUDSON.
I NEVER JOKE ABOUT SEA MONSTERS, DARLING.
SO YOU DIDN'T SEE WHO SHOT YOU AT ALL? NOTHING?
NOTHING. SWORD OR AXE, JONES?
UH. YOU PICK.
YOU LOOK LIKE AN AXE GIRL TO ME.
...THANK YOU?
WHAT ABOUT THAT COOL MORNINGSTAR THING?
OH ☠☠☠☠ NO, JONES. YOU'RE NOT READY FOR THAT ☠☠☠☠.
SO...ANYTHING I SHOULD KNOW?
CHOP HARD AT ANYTHING THAT DOESN'T LOOK LIKE ME OR A CIVILIAN.
IS IT REALLY GOING AFTER CIVILIANS?
WELL, I DON'T THINK IT'S MAKING ITS WAY TOWARD THE PIER FOR ☠☠☠☠ AND GIGGLES, NOW IS IT, DARLING?
FAIR ENOUGH.
I SORT OF LIKE HER.
A LOT.

SO...IT'S POSSIBLE I'M ANGRIER ABOUT BEING SHOT IN THE HEAD THAN I REALIZED BECAUSE THIS FEELS *GREAT.*
DOWNRIGHT CATHARTIC, EVEN.
SLUICE
HOW MANY OF THEM ARE THERE IN HERE, ANYWAY?
UNCLEAR. AND PACE YOURSELF, JONES, OTHERWISE YOU'RE NOT GOING TO BE ABLE TO LIFT YOUR ARMS IN AN HOUR.
THIS IS GOING TO TAKE *AN HOUR?*
ONLY IF WE'RE BLOODY LUCKY, DARLING.
SLICE
I HOPE I'VE GOT ENOUGH RAGE AND GUILT TO POWER ME FOR AN HOUR.
WHO AM I KIDDING? I'LL BE FINE.
CHOP
SO YOU *REALLY* DIDN'T SEE THE SHOOTER.
FOR THE LAST TIME, JONES, NO. IF I HAD, THEY WOULDN'T BE BLOODY BREATHING, WOULD THEY?
HAVE YOU EVER MET A GIRL NAMED DIA SLOANE?
...HOLY I DID.
JACKPOT.

DON'T TELL ME SHE DID IT. THAT SWEET THING? CAN'T BE. SHE BEGGED ME TO KILL HER. SHE'S NO BLOODY KILLER.
WELL, EXCEPT OF HERSELF MAYBE.
SMACK
SHE WANTED YOU TO KILL HER?
THE PLOT THICKENS.
BAM
CAME TO ME SOMETHING LIKE A YEAR AGO. BEGGING, LITERALLY IN TEARS.
SOMETHING ABOUT HOW SHE WAS A MONSTER AND SHE KNEW I KILLED MONSTERS AND WOULD I KILL HER.
INTERESTING. COMES TO ME TO FIND DIRT ON THE BOYFRIEND. TO ELSA FOR A MERCY KILLING.
AND BOTH OF US FAILED TO HELP HER. AND NOW SHE'S DEAD.
SQUISH
AND YOU DIDN'T KILL HER, OBVIOUSLY.
GIVE ME SOME CREDIT, JONES.
WAS SHE ONE?
A MONSTER?
YEAH.
KRAK

DEPENDS ON YOUR POINT OF VIEW, I SUPPOSE. WE'RE ALL MONSTERS, AREN'T WE?
ELSA. MAYBE IT'S BECAUSE I WAS SHOT IN THE HEAD RECENTLY, BUT I'M NOT FEELING REAL EXISTENTIAL RIGHT NOW. CAN YOU PLEASE JUST ANSWER THE GODDAMN QUESTION?
FAIR ENOUGH.
SMASH
HARD TO SAY WHAT SHE IS, JONES, AND I'M NOT TRYING TO BE DEEP. SHE CERTAINLY ISN'T SOME MINDLESS SEA MONSTER INTENT ON EATING NEW YORK LIKE THIS MOTHER☠☠☠☠☠☠.
THUNK
AND NOW WE SEE HOW ELSA REACTS TO THIS...
WASN'T.
WASN'T?
DIA'S DEAD.
☠☠☠☠☠. REALLY?
INTERESTING.

WELL, I'M STILL INVESTIGATING. THERE ARE OBVIOUSLY SOME ODDITIES SURROUNDING THE CASE.
BUT YES, I FOUND HER BODY ON MY OFFICE FLOOR ON SATURDAY MORNING.
YEAH. THAT USUALLY SEALS IT. BUT YOU STILL NEED TO INVESTIGATE? NO OFFENSE, JONES, BUT YOU MIGHT BE IN THE WRONG LINE OF WORK.
THUNK
GOOD NEWS IS YOU THROW A MEAN AXE.
KRAK
I'VE CALLED SEVERAL TIMES TO MAKE SURE HER CORPSE IS STILL AT THE MORGUE. UNLIKE US, SHE APPEARS TO BE STAYING DEAD.
BUT SHE'S STILL THE CONNECTING THREAD IN ALL OF THIS. SO I'M FOLLOWING THAT THREAD.
SQUELCH
OKAY. I BUY THAT.
SO WHAT'S THE QUESTION?
WHAT IS THE QUESTION?
RIGHT.
WHEN YOU MET HER, WHEN SHE THOUGHT SHE WAS A MONSTER...WHAT MADE HER THINK THAT? DID SHE HAVE POWERS?

HARD TO REMEMBER. IT WAS MORE THAN A YEAR AGO. SHE SAID SOMETHING ABOUT... WHAT WAS IT? BEING CAREFUL WHAT SHE WISHED FOR.
YEAH. THAT WAS IT. NOT TRUSTING HER THOUGHTS.
SQUICK
HOW DID IT END?
I TALKED SOME BLOODY SENSE INTO HER, GAVE HER SOME TEA... OR MAYBE SOME WHISKY...MAYBE BOTH.
PUT HER IN A CAB, NEVER HEARD FROM HER AGAIN.
DO ME A FAVOR, JONES.
LET ME KNOW ABOUT DIA'S FUNERAL. I'D LIKE TO GO...I COULD HAVE DONE MORE FOR HER.
SURE.
ME TOO.
YOU EVER GIVE UP THE BADGE, OR WHATEVER IT IS THAT P.I.s HAVE, LET ME KNOW. I CAN ALWAYS USE A WOMAN WHO'S GOOD WITH A MOTHER-☠☠☠☠☠☠☠ AXE.
DEAL.
SERIAL KILLER. TRIED TO KILL FOUR WOMEN IN AS MANY DAYS.
NO. SCRATCH THAT.
HE *DID* KILL FOUR. TWO OF US LIVED ANYWAY.
TIME TO FIGURE OUT WHY THE OTHER TWO DIDN'T.

TIME: MONDAY, 10:59 PM
LOCATION: HELL'S KITCHEN
The Menagerie
WHITE RABBIT'S CLUB, THE MENAGERIE. NAMED AFTER AN OLD SUPER VILLAIN TEAM...OR A CURRENT ONE. IT'S HARD TO KEEP TRACK.
HEY. SO I WAS HOPING--
YOU'RE IN.
OH. OKAY, THEN. THANKS.
IT'S THE PANTS. BOUNCERS LOVE THE LEATHER PANTS.
OR MAYBE IT'S THE WET T-SHIRT.
HAVE YOU SEEN THIS WOMAN AROUND THE CLUB? HER HAIR MIGHT BE LESS GREEN NOW...AND A DIFFERENT CUT.
SORRY THE PICTURE'S WET. IT'S BEEN A LONG NIGHT.
SHE LOOKS FAMILIAR, BUT I CAN'T BE SURE. I SEE A LOT OF PEOPLE.
WHAT ABOUT HER BOYFRIEND?
OH, *THAT* JACKASS.
YEAH. OKAY. I'VE SEEN A GIRL THAT LOOKS A LITTLE LIKE THAT WITH THAT GUY.
ANY PARTICULAR REASON YOU REMEMBER HIM?
WHITE RABBIT THREW HIM OUT TWO WEEKS AGO. OR RATHER, SHE HAD ME DO IT.
AND THERE'S MOTIVE.

YOU KNOW WHY SHE EJECTED HIM?
NO, MA'AM. SHE DIDN'T EXACTLY SHARE HER EVERY THOUGHT.
THANK GOD.
ARE YOU EVEN GOING IN?
UH. YEAH. ONE MORE QUESTION.
YOU EVER SEE SKEIN AROUND HERE? SHE'S A SUPER VILLAIN... OR MAYBE FORMER VILLAIN?
YEAH, SHE USED TO COME IN. NICE GIRL. DESERVED BETTER THAN SHE GOT.
YOU KNOW WHAT HAPPENED TO HER?
OF COURSE. IT HAPPENED UPSTAIRS. TWO DAYS AFTER THE RABBIT. SAME AS THE RABBIT...BULLET TO THE BACK OF THE HEAD.
AND THOSE WERE NOT EASY WOMEN TO KILL.
DID SKEIN KNOW THE JACKASS TOO?
NOT THAT I KNOW OF. TALK TO ANNA AT THE BAR. SHE'S THE CAT.
ALL RIGHT. THANKS.
SO WE JUST WENT WITH THE LITERAL MENAGERIE THING, THEN. CLASSY.
IS THAT GIRL SUPPOSED TO BE A PEACOCK...? Y'KNOW WHAT? I DON'T EVEN WANT TO KNOW.

ARE YOU ANNA?
YEAH. WHY?

THE BOUNCER TOLD ME YOU KNEW SKEIN AND MIGHT TALK TO ME.
I DON'T KNOW. I DIDN'T SEE ANYTHING. I WASN'T EVEN WORKING THAT NIGHT.
LISTEN, I'M SORRY. I'M A P.I., AND I'M TRYING TO FIGURE OUT WHO KILLED HER.

IT HAPPENED IN THE CLUB, RIGHT? HOW IS IT STILL OPEN?
IT WAS UPSTAIRS. THE COPS BLOCKED IT OFF. RABBIT'S BUSINESS PARTNERS DIDN'T WANT TO CLOSE. DICKS.
YOU WERE FRIENDS WITH HER?

YEAH. I MEAN, PEOPLE SAY THAT RABBIT WAS CRAZY, BUT SHE WAS SMART AND SHE DIDN'T TAKE CRAP FROM ANYONE. I DIDN'T KNOW SKEIN AS WELL, BUT SHE SEEMED THE SAME.
I LIKED THEM.

BOUNCER SAID THEY HAD AN INCIDENT WITH A GUY NAMED JARED?
UGH. THAT GUY. HE HIT ON RABBIT A COUPLE TIMES BEFORE SHE THREW HIM OUT.
DO YOU THINK HE WOULD HAVE COME BACK LOOKING FOR REVENGE?

WAIT. YOU THINK *HE* KILLED THEM? NO WAY. HE COULDN'T HAVE TAKEN EITHER OF THEM ON HIS BEST DAY.
WHITE RABBIT DIDN'T EXACTLY HAVE SUPER-POWERS, BUT SHE WAS A BADASS.
AND SKEIN... I MEAN, SHE HAD LEGIT POWERS...THAT THING WHERE YOU CAN MOVE SHIT WITH YOUR MIND?

NO WAY THAT DOUCHE COULD TAKE THEM OUT.
IS IT POSSIBLE JARED HAD POWERS?
HE DIDN'T SEEM LIKE A GUY WHO'D BE SHY ABOUT SHOWING OFF POWERS, Y'KNOW?

IF YOU THINK OF ANYTHING ELSE, OR IF HE COMES BACK, GIVE ME A CALL.
SURE. BUT NO WAY STUART WOULD LET HIM BACK IN HERE.
STUART?
THE BOUNCER.
ALIAS INVESTIGATIONS

HEYYYYYY, BAAAAABY.
NOPE.
ANNNND THAT'S MY CUE TO GO HOME.

WAY TOO CLOSE, GUY. BACK OFF.
DON' BE LIKE THAT. YOU'RE SO CUTE, WE SHOULD BE FRIENDS.
THAT'S NOT GONNA HAPPEN. STEP BACK.

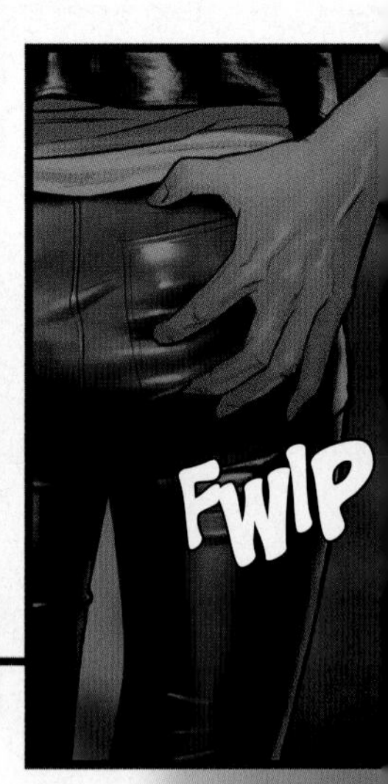
FWIP

BOOM

A SLIIIIGHT OVERREACTION PERHAPS.

BUT I'M PISSED.
THAS RIGHT, WALK AWAY, YOU FEM'NIST *BITCH*.
MAYBE MORE PISSED THAN I REALIZED.
AND I'M GODDAMN SICK OF DUDES JUST PUTTING THEIR HANDS WHEREVER THEY WANT.
DUDES THINKING THEY CAN JUST *DO* WHATEVER THEY WANT.

FEMINIST BITCHES.
ALL FOUR VICTIMS WERE POWERFUL. IN FACT, THE EXACT KINDS OF WOMEN THAT DRIVE CERTAIN KINDS OF DUDES CRAZY.
ALL FOUR VICTIMS CAME INTO CONTACT WITH DIA OR JARED. TWO OF US TRIED BUT FAILED TO HELP DIA, AND WE'RE STILL ALIVE. THE TWO THAT HAD DIRECT CONFRONTATIONS WITH JARED...ARE DEAD. THAT SEEMS HARD TO IGNORE.
ELSA AND I ARE ALSO THE TWO MOST RECENT VICTIMS... MAYBE THE KILLER IS GETTING WORSE? THEY USUALLY GET BETTER, THOUGH, NOT WORSE.
TIME: MONDAY, 11:58 PM
LOCATION: ALIAS INVESTIGATIONS
MAYBE THERE *IS* SOMETHING MAGICAL ABOUT WHAT THE KILLER IS DOING AND IT'S WEARING OFF?
DOCTOR STRANGE SAID THE *BULLET* WASN'T MAGICAL, BUT HE SAID I HAD BEEN TOUCHED BY SOMETHING SUPERNATURAL.
MAYBE WHATEVER FORCE IS ALLOWING THIS PERSON TO KILL IS LOSING ITS POTENCY?
OR MAYBE IT *IS* SOMETHING TO DO WITH DIA? CONTACT WITH HER SOMEHOW PROTECTED THOSE OF US WHO KNEW HER?
BUT IT DIDN'T *FEEL* LIKE I WAS PROTECTED FROM DEATH. NO. I *WAS* DEAD. AND THEN I WASN'T. ELSA SAID THE SAME.
IF IT *IS* SOMETHING THAT'S WEARING OFF, THEN WE'RE LESS LIKELY TO HAVE ANY MORE SUCCESSFUL MURDERS...
...BUT I CAN'T JUST WAIT AROUND HOPING TO GET LUCKY.
DIA REMAINS THE KEY, THE THREAD THAT CONNECTS ALL OF THIS. I JUST HAVE TO KEEP DIGGING UNTIL I HIT SOMETHING.
WELL. *THAT* IS WHAT WE CALL A GODDAMN LEAD.

BANG BANG BANG
JONES! OPEN UP!

MISTY KNIGHT, CURRENTLY OF THE FBI'S NEW "ABERRANT CRIMES DIVISION," BANGING ON MY DOOR AT THREE A.M., CANNOT POSSIBLY BE GOOD.
WHIR
CLICK CLICK
HRRRMMMM

JONES!
HRRRMMMM WHIR
CLICK CLICK

JONES! GODDAMMIT, I *WILL* BREAK IN. DON'T TEST ME.
WITH THAT TONE OF VOICE, MISTY WANTS ONE OF A FEW THINGS, NONE OF THEM PLEASANT FOR ME OR HELPFUL TO *MY* INVESTIGATION.

I'M NOT SHARING WHAT I FOUND WITH HER.
NOR AM I WAITING TO FOLLOW UP THIS LEAD.
I DON'T HAVE TIME FOR MORE ROUNDS WITH MISTY OVER THE SAME OLD BULLSHIT.

YEAH. CATCH ME NOW, KNIGHT. I'D LIKE TO SEE THAT.
THERE'S MY CAR.
FORGOT WHERE I LEFT IT.
THAT WAS ACTUALLY PRETTY GREAT. A TOP TEN LANDING AT LEAST. MAYBE I'M GETTING BETTER AT IT. IS THAT POSSIBLE?
NAH.
MA'AM, DID YOU JUST BREAK OUR SIDEWALK?
NOPE. WASN'T ME.

BREAKING AND ENTERING IS BECOMING A BAD HABIT OF MINE.
CRUNCH
PHOTO OF DIA AND MEATBALL. GOOD TO KNOW I STILL KNOW HOW TO FIND PEOPLE. OR AT LEAST WHERE THEY *USED* TO BE.
I ALWAYS FELT EARLY-MORNING HOURS SHOULD BE LESS CREEPY THAN THE MIDDLE OF THE NIGHT.
BUT THAT'S DUMB. IT'S NOT LIKE LIGHT CHANGES ANYTHING. BAD THINGS HAPPEN IN DAYLIGHT TOO.
BAD THINGS HAPPEN ALL THE TIME.
BAD THINGS DON'T CARE ABOUT ANY OTHER THINGS.

NOT THIS TIME, YOU SONOFABITCH.
SKRRRRICT

?!
DIA.

4

TIME: UNKNOWN
LOCATION: UNKNOWN
TIME IS WHAT I'M WORRIED ABOUT. AT FIRST I THOUGHT, SO LONG AS HE'S HERE, HE'S NOT HURTING ANYONE, SO WHAT'S THE HARM?

BUT HE'S TOO CONTROLLED TO NOT HAVE A PLAN. HE DOESN'T CARE THAT HE'S WASTING TIME... IT'S WHAT HE WANTS.
AND THAT'S NO GOOD FOR ME.
YOU SEE, IT'S CLEAR TO ME WHAT YOUR PROBLEM IS, EVEN IF YOU CAN'T SEE IT.
OH?

YEAH. YOU WANT TO HEAR IT?
NOT REALLY, BUT I HAVEN'T BEEN ABLE TO SHUT YOU UP SO FAR, SO GO AHEAD. KNOCK YOURSELF OUT.
YOUR PROBLEM IS FEAR.
HEH. YOU THINK SO?
I REALLY DO.

COULDN'T BE MORE WRONG. BUT I THINK, SOON ENOUGH, FEAR WILL BE *YOUR* PROBLEM, JONES.
GUESS WE'LL SEE, HUH?

TIME: TUESDAY, 5:01 AM
LOCATION: COLD SPRING, NY
CURRENT LOCATION OF DIA SLOANE
YOU LOOK PRETTY GOOD FOR A CORPSE, DIA.
→KOFF← H-HE DIDN'T FOLLOW YOU, DID HE?
WHO?
JARED.
NOT DEAD.
NO. JARED DID NOT FOLLOW ME.
ALSO RELEVANT... YOU'RE NOT DEAD. BUT OF COURSE YOU'RE NOT, NOBODY KNOWS HOW TO STAY DEAD ANYMORE.
I CAN EXPLAIN?
DAMN RIGHT YOU WILL.
I'M WAITING.

→KOFF←...H-HOW DID YOU FIND ME? MY NAME'S NOT ON THE LEASE AND I PAY CASH, IT'S ALL VERY SHADY... →KOFF← THOUGHT THAT WOULD KEEP ME HIDDEN. →KOFF←
"NEW" GREEN HAIR.
DEVELOPING BRUISE.
TATTOO.
OBSCURE BAND. AGAIN.
I FOUND PHOTOS OF YOUR CAT MEATBALL ON QUIKPIK.
FROM THERE I WAS ABLE TO PULL A PARTIAL PHONE NUMBER OFF HIS TAGS.
I CAME UP WITH SIX POSSIBLE NUMBERS FOR YOU AND TRACKED THOSE TO ADDRESSES. THIS WAS ONE OF THEM.
WAS GOING TO SPEND TODAY CHECKING THEM ALL OUT. AND THEN THIS...
...INTERACTIVE MAPS PHOTO NARROWED IT DOWN RATHER DRAMATICALLY.
→KOFF← F-FOILED BY TAKING OUT THE TRASH. →KOFF← NO GOOD DEED, I GUESS.
IT TOOK ALL OF A DAY, SO YOU BETTER HOPE JARED IS A LOT DUMBER THAN I AM.
IF IT →KOFF← IF IT ONLY TOOK YOU A DAY, THEN HOW COME YOU DIDN'T FIND ME LAST TIME I DISAPPEARED?
I'VE BEEN ASKING MYSELF THAT A LOT IN THE LAST 72 HOURS.
I FAILED YOU PRETTY HARD BACK THEN AND I COULD OFFER UP A LOT OF EXCUSES, BUT NONE OF THEM MATTER. ALL I CAN SAY IS THAT I'M SORRY.
I DIDN'T MEAN--
IT'S FINE. YOU HAVE EVERY RIGHT TO SAY THAT TO ME. BUT IN THE LAST THREE DAYS, I FOUND YOUR CORPSE ON MY OFFICE FLOOR...
...WAS ARRESTED FOR YOUR MURDER...
...GOT SHOT IN THE BACK OF THE HEAD...
...DIED...
...CAME BACK TO LIFE...
...WAS INTERROGATED BY AN FBI AGENT WHO HATES ME...
...WENT HIP-DEEP IN SEA MONSTERS IN THE HUDSON RIVER...
...AND WAS HIT ON BY A DRUNKEN PERV.
ALL WHILE BEING WRACKED WITH GUILT OVER YOUR DEATH AND THE FACT THAT I FAILED YOU WHEN YOU CAME TO ME YEARS AGO FOR HELP.
AND I'M SORRY ABOUT YOUR NECK. I DIDN'T MEAN TO HURT YOU...BUT I'M A BIT ON EDGE WHEN APPROACHED FROM BEHIND THESE DAYS.
AND I NEED YOU TO START TALKING.

OKAY. W-WHERE DO I START? ≻KOFF≺
JARED. WHEN DID YOU MEET JARED? REFRESH MY MEMORY.

I FEEL LIKE I'VE KNOWN HIM MY WHOLE LIFE. I SUPPOSE THAT'S PART OF THE PROBLEM.
WE WERE HIGH SCHOOL SWEETHEARTS. AND IT WAS SWEET. THAT'S THE PERFECT WORD.

AND WHEN YOU CAME TO ME, LOOKING FOR DIRT ON HIM, HE WASN'T SO SWEET ANYMORE?

...NO. HE'D ALWAYS BEEN LIKE THAT. SWEETEST GUY AROUND. UNLESS...
UNLESS HE GOT MAD.
...YES.
SO THEN... HE GOT POWERS OF SOME KIND AND THINGS GOT WORSE.

...

NO. THE POWERS ARE MINE. I'M THE MONSTER HERE.

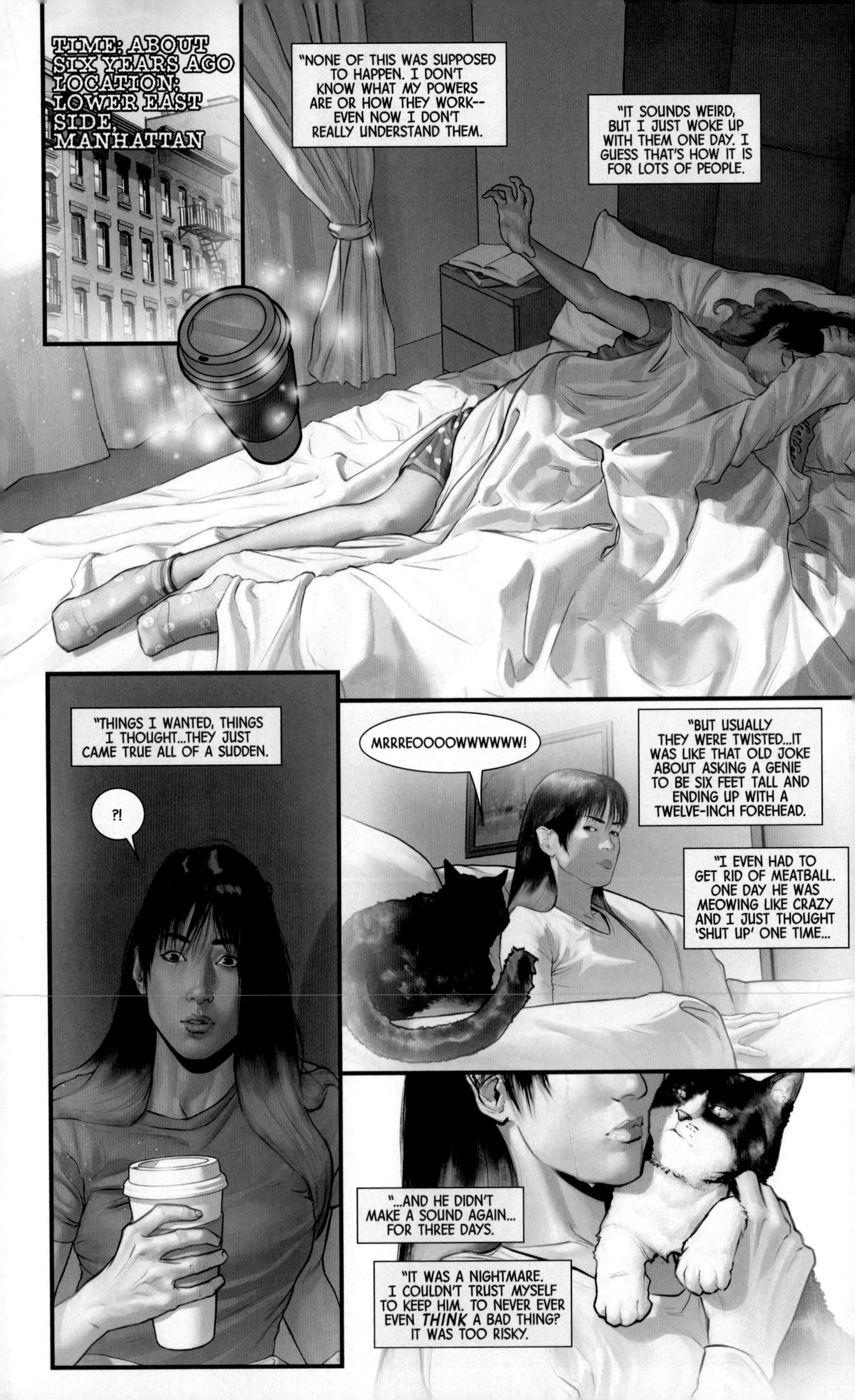
TIME: ABOUT SIX YEARS AGO
LOCATION: LOWER EAST SIDE, MANHATTAN
"NONE OF THIS WAS SUPPOSED TO HAPPEN. I DON'T KNOW WHAT MY POWERS ARE OR HOW THEY WORK-- EVEN NOW I DON'T REALLY UNDERSTAND THEM.
"IT SOUNDS WEIRD, BUT I JUST WOKE UP WITH THEM ONE DAY. I GUESS THAT'S HOW IT IS FOR LOTS OF PEOPLE.
"THINGS I WANTED, THINGS I THOUGHT...THEY JUST CAME TRUE ALL OF A SUDDEN.
?!
MRRREOOOOWWWWWW!
"BUT USUALLY THEY WERE TWISTED...IT WAS LIKE THAT OLD JOKE ABOUT ASKING A GENIE TO BE SIX FEET TALL AND ENDING UP WITH A TWELVE-INCH FOREHEAD.
"I EVEN HAD TO GET RID OF MEATBALL. ONE DAY HE WAS MEOWING LIKE CRAZY AND I JUST THOUGHT 'SHUT UP' ONE TIME...
"...AND HE DIDN'T MAKE A SOUND AGAIN... FOR THREE DAYS.
"IT WAS A NIGHTMARE. I COULDN'T TRUST MYSELF TO KEEP HIM. TO NEVER EVER EVEN *THINK* A BAD THING? IT WAS TOO RISKY.

"BUT THINGS WITH JARED GOT WORSE AND WORSE. HE RESENTED THE POWER I HAD, EVEN THOUGH IT WAS MESSING MY LIFE UP.
"HE COULDN'T HANDLE IT. I--I DON'T KNOW WHAT IT WAS ABOUT ME HAVING POWER, BUT HE JUST...I DON'T KNOW, IT MADE HIM SO ANGRY.
"AND ALL I COULD THINK WAS THAT IF HE HAD POWER LIKE ME, THINGS WOULD BE BETTER--THAT WOULD MAKE HIM HAPPY, THAT WOULD MAKE THINGS LIKE THEY USED TO BE."
OH MY GOD. HE GOT THE POWER FROM *YOU*. YOU *GAVE* IT TO HIM.
...YES. I DIDN'T MEAN FOR IT TO HAPPEN, BUT YES. THAT'S EXACTLY WHAT I DID.
AND THINGS DIDN'T GET BETTER.
NO. THINGS ONLY GOT WORSE. AND EVENTUALLY I HAD TO RUN FROM HIM.

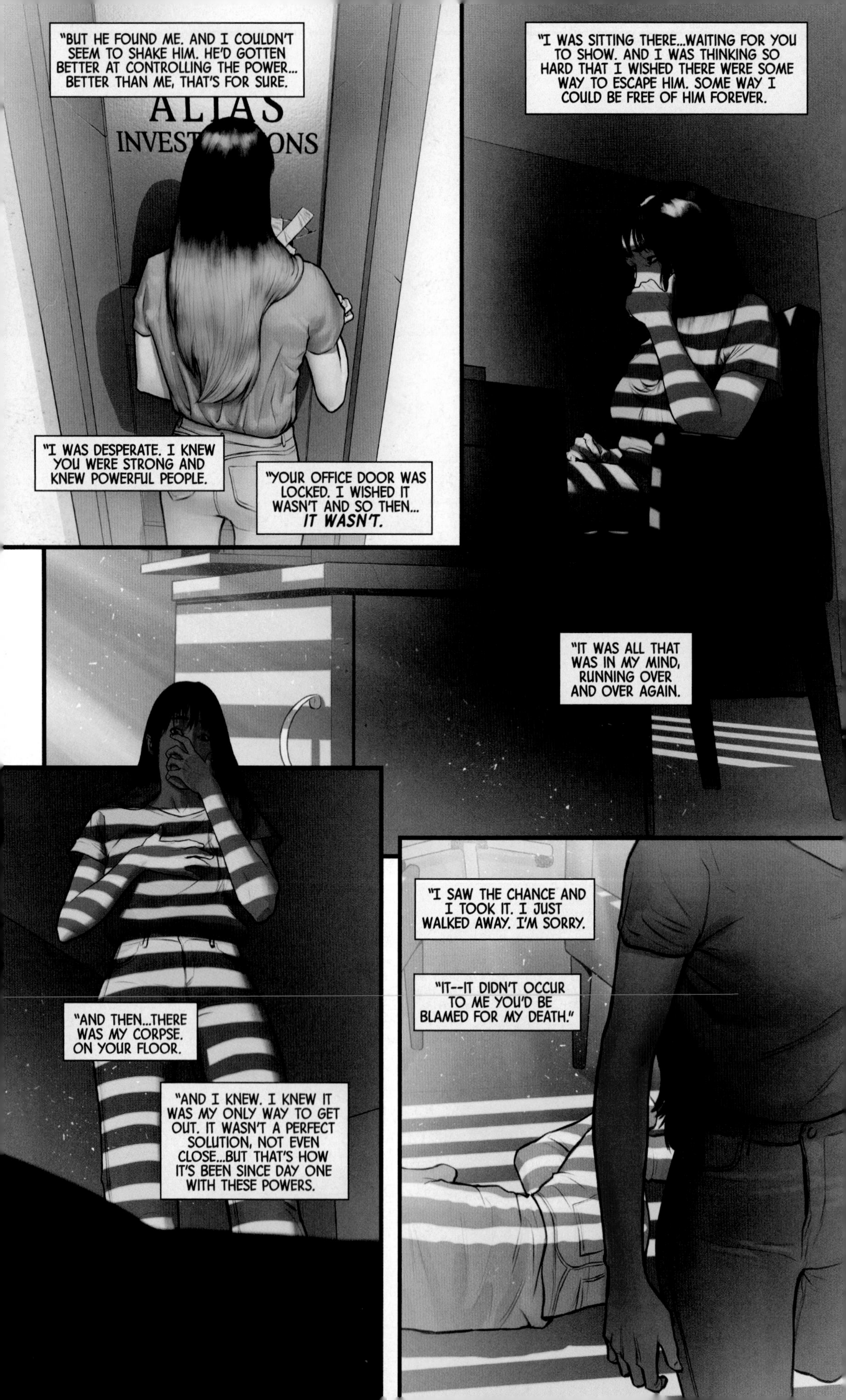
"BUT HE FOUND ME. AND I COULDN'T SEEM TO SHAKE HIM. HE'D GOTTEN BETTER AT CONTROLLING THE POWER... BETTER THAN ME, THAT'S FOR SURE.
"I WAS DESPERATE. I KNEW YOU WERE STRONG AND KNEW POWERFUL PEOPLE.
"YOUR OFFICE DOOR WAS LOCKED. I WISHED IT WASN'T AND SO THEN... *IT WASN'T.*
"I WAS SITTING THERE...WAITING FOR YOU TO SHOW. AND I WAS THINKING SO HARD THAT I WISHED THERE WERE SOME WAY TO ESCAPE HIM. SOME WAY I COULD BE FREE OF HIM FOREVER.
"IT WAS ALL THAT WAS IN MY MIND, RUNNING OVER AND OVER AGAIN.
"AND THEN...THERE WAS MY CORPSE. ON YOUR FLOOR.
"AND I KNEW. I KNEW IT WAS MY ONLY WAY TO GET OUT. IT WASN'T A PERFECT SOLUTION, NOT EVEN CLOSE...BUT THAT'S HOW IT'S BEEN SINCE DAY ONE WITH THESE POWERS.
"I SAW THE CHANCE AND I TOOK IT. I JUST WALKED AWAY. I'M SORRY.
"IT--IT DIDN'T OCCUR TO ME YOU'D BE BLAMED FOR MY DEATH."

YOU DON'T KNOW HOW THE COPS HAPPENED TO SHOW UP, THEN?
NO. MAYBE JARED WAS FOLLOWING ME, AND HE CALLED IT IN. MAYBE TO SET YOU UP OR MAYBE NOT, I DON'T KNOW.
OKAY. WELL, THAT'S A HELL OF A STORY, DIA. AND YOU'RE NOT GONNA WANT TO HEAR THIS, BUT YOU GOTTA COME BACK WITH ME TO MANHATTAN.
NO GODDAMN WAY.
HE'LL KILL ME.
YES. JARED IS KILLING WOMEN, DIA. AND YOU'RE RESPONSIBLE FOR GIVING HIM THE POWER TO DO IT, ACCIDENT OR NO. I NEED YOU TO HELP ME CORRECT THAT.
HE'LL TRY. BUT WE'RE NOT GOING TO LET THAT HAPPEN.
HE KILLED YOU. HOW ARE YOU GOING TO STOP HIM?
THE POWER CAME FROM YOU. YOU'RE STRONGER THAN HE IS. AND I KNOW A LOT OF PEOPLE WITH A LOT OF POWER WHO CAN HELP YOU, EVEN IF I CAN'T.
LET ME GIVE YOU ANOTHER REASON... YOU EVER WANT TO BE IN A RELATIONSHIP AGAIN? YOU GOTTA FACE IT HEAD-ON AND LEARN TO TAKE CONTROL OF YOUR LIFE. TRUST ME. I KNOW THIS... INTIMATELY.
...
HOW ABOUT SEEING YOUR CAT AGAIN? YOU WANT TO SEE YOUR CAT AGAIN, YOU GOTTA LEARN TO CONTROL THIS THING.

TIME: FIVE MINUTES LATER
LOCATION: JESSICA'S CAR
WELL, THAT DIDN'T WORK.
PING PING
OH MY GOD.
--CRIME HAS DEVASTATED THE CITY. SUCH AN ICONIC YOUNG WOMAN LOST TO US FAR TOO SOON.
THE NYPD HAS OFFERED NO COMMENT ON THE PUBLIC SPECULATION THAT THIS MIGHT BE CONNECTED TO ATTEMPTS ON THE LIVES OF TWO OTHER HIGH-PROFILE NEW YORKERS-- JESSICA JONES AND ELSA BLOODSTONE.
WE'LL HAVE MORE AS THIS STORY DEVELOPS THROUGHOUT THE DAY...
TIME: TUESDAY, 7:55 AM
LOCATION: UPPER WEST SIDE, MANHATTAN
IF THIS IS HIM...AND OF COURSE IT IS...HE'S DEFINITELY MOVING UP IN THE WORLD.
NYPD

WELL, WELL, WELL. THE POWER OF CATS, I SWEAR TO GOD.
I CHANGED MY MIND.
I SEE THAT. AND I APPRECIATE IT.
HOW DID YOU GET HERE?
WELL...I SAID I WASN'T GOOD AT MY POWER, I DIDN'T SAY I HADN'T BEEN PRACTICING.
YOU WISHED YOURSELF HERE? WOW. THAT'S INCREDIBLE, DIA.
THANKS. BUT... THIS ISN'T YOUR OFFICE...WHERE ARE WE?
WELL, DON'T FREAK OUT...BUT THERE'S BEEN ANOTHER MURDER.
OH GOD. HE COULD BE *HERE.*
I...I HAD THIS INVISIBILITY THING I WAS TRYING... BUT I--I THINK I'D HAVE TO CALM DOWN FIRST...
PROBABLY NOT. JUST STAY IN THE CAR AND WAIT FOR ME.
DEFINITELY CALM DOWN BEFORE YOU TRY ANYTHING WITH INVISIBILITY.
TWENTY MINUTES, OKAY?
O-OKAY.
OH GOD.
PETER.
GONNA HAVE TO BLUFF HARDER THAN I'VE EVER BLUFFED BEFORE...OR MAYBE I'LL SEE A FRIENDLY FACE?

SPIDER-MAN?
JESSICA... HI...
ARE YOU... ARE YOU OKAY? I--I DON'T THINK YOU SHOULD BE HERE.
SHE'S DEAD, YOU KNOW.
...
HE'S IN SHOCK.
MARY JANE IS DEAD.

I CAN'T TELL HIM I CAN GET HER BACK. CAN'T GET HIS HOPES UP IN ASE I'M WRONG.
HE LOVED HER, IF NOT NOW, THEN BEFORE. AND FROM THE LOOKS OF HIM, IT'S STILL NOW. IT'S ALWAYS.
AND THAT MEANS AS SOON AS THE SHOCK WEARS OFF HE'S GOING TO DO SOMETHING VERY, VERY STUPID.
PUNCH A COP...TAKE OFF HIS MASK...KILL A BAD GUY... I DON'T EVEN KNOW. WHAT WOULD I DO IF IT WERE LUKE UP THERE?
I'D TRY TO TEAR THE SUN FROM THE SKY. ONCE I COULD FEEL ANYTHING.
PETER. YOU CAN'T BE HERE RIGHT NOW.
I...I--I DON'T KNOW WHAT TO DO? I ALWAYS KNOW WHAT TO DO...
...BUT NOW IT'S LIKE THERE'S THIS--THIS NOISE IN MY HEAD...
YOU'RE GOING TO DO WHAT I TELL YOU TO DO.
YOU'RE GOING TO GO HOME.
AND I'M GOING TO GO UP THERE AND FIND OUT WHAT HAPPENED. AND I'M GOING TO CALL YOU VERY SOON.
I SHOULD LEAVE? IS THAT RIGHT?
YES. JUST FOR NOW.
...OKAY.
I HOPE HE MAKES IT HOME BEFORE THE SHOCK WEARS OFF. I'VE NEVER... I'VE NEVER SEEN HIM LIKE THAT BEFORE.

WHOOSH
→HUFF←
NAILED IT.
IF I HAVE TO DROP MISTY KNIGHT'S NAME TO GET IN THERE, IT'S GOING TO KILL ME INSIDE.
OH, THANK THE GODS FOR INCOMPETENT COPS.

TIME: TUESDAY, 8:07 AM
LOCATION: APARTMENT OF MARY JANE WATSON
JESUS. I AM IN THE WRONG LINE OF WORK.
THAT GUY...CALL IT P.I.-SENSE IF YOU LIKE, BUT... SOMETHING'S NOT RIGHT ABOUT THAT GUY.
HEY! GET AWAY FROM HER!
I--I CAN'T.
I SAID BACK OFF!
Y-YOU DON'T UNDERSTAND...
LIKE HELL I DON'T... JARED.
Y-YOU HAVE TO L-LET ME FINISH!
GOD. LOOK AT HER. SHE'S ICONIC. SHE'S MAGNIFICENT. AND...SHE'S REALLY DEAD.
I--I'M TRYING TO FIX IT...FIX HER... LIKE I FIXED YOU.

WAIT. WHAT?
I...HE SHOT YOU...AND I--I MADE IT LIKE IT DIDN'T HAPPEN. I--I CAN DO IT AGAIN... BUT YOU HAVE TO LET ME FINISH.
...FINISH.
I THINK I HAVE TO LET HIM TRY... IT'S NOT LIKE HE CAN MAKE IT WORSE...SHE'S ALREADY DEAD.
AND SOMETHING BROUGHT *ME* BACK. ELSA TOO. MAYBE THIS WAS IT?
I'VE BEEN LOOKING FOR JARED THE KILLER...BUT IS IT POSSIBLE HE'S BEEN JARED THE SAVIOR ALL ALONG?
KOFF
HOLY SHIT. SHE'S ALIVE.
YOU DID IT.
JARED, WHAT THE *HELL* IS GOING ON?
IT'S SO COMPLICATED.
I BUY THAT. BUT START TALKING ANYWAY.
UM. CAN SOMEONE UNZIP ME?

GO EASY.
HOLY SHIT. SHE'S ALIVE.
UM. SEND UP THE KIT RIGHT AWAY. AND NOTIFY THE COPS TO GET UP HERE IMMEDIATELY. SOMETHING'S HAPPENED.
MISS WATSON, YOU REALLY MUST LET US PUT YOU ON THE STRETCHER TO TAKE YOU DOWNSTAIRS.
GUYS, I JUST GOT UNZIPPED FROM A BODY BAG... I'M NOT LYING DOWN AGAIN FOR A MONTH. IF YOU INSIST ON DOING MORE TESTS, I'M FREAKING WALKING DOWNSTAIRS ON MY OWN POWER.
OFFICER BRENTLY. YOU'RE NEEDED DOWNSTAIRS ASAP.
GREAT.
YOU TWO STAY PUT. I'LL BE RIGHT BACK. WE'RE NOT EVEN CLOSE TO DONE HERE.
I'VE...I'VE BEEN TRYING TO FIX THE BAD THINGS HE DOES...BUT I DIDN'T KNOW AT FIRST...AND I WAS TOO LATE FOR SOME OF THEM.
WHITE RABBIT AND SKEIN.
...AND DIA.
HE DOESN'T KNOW SHE'S ALIVE. GOTTA KEEP THAT IN MY POCKET FOR NOW.
HE'S A MONSTER. HE'S EVERYTHING ROTTEN. EVERYTHING I DON'T WANT TO BE--

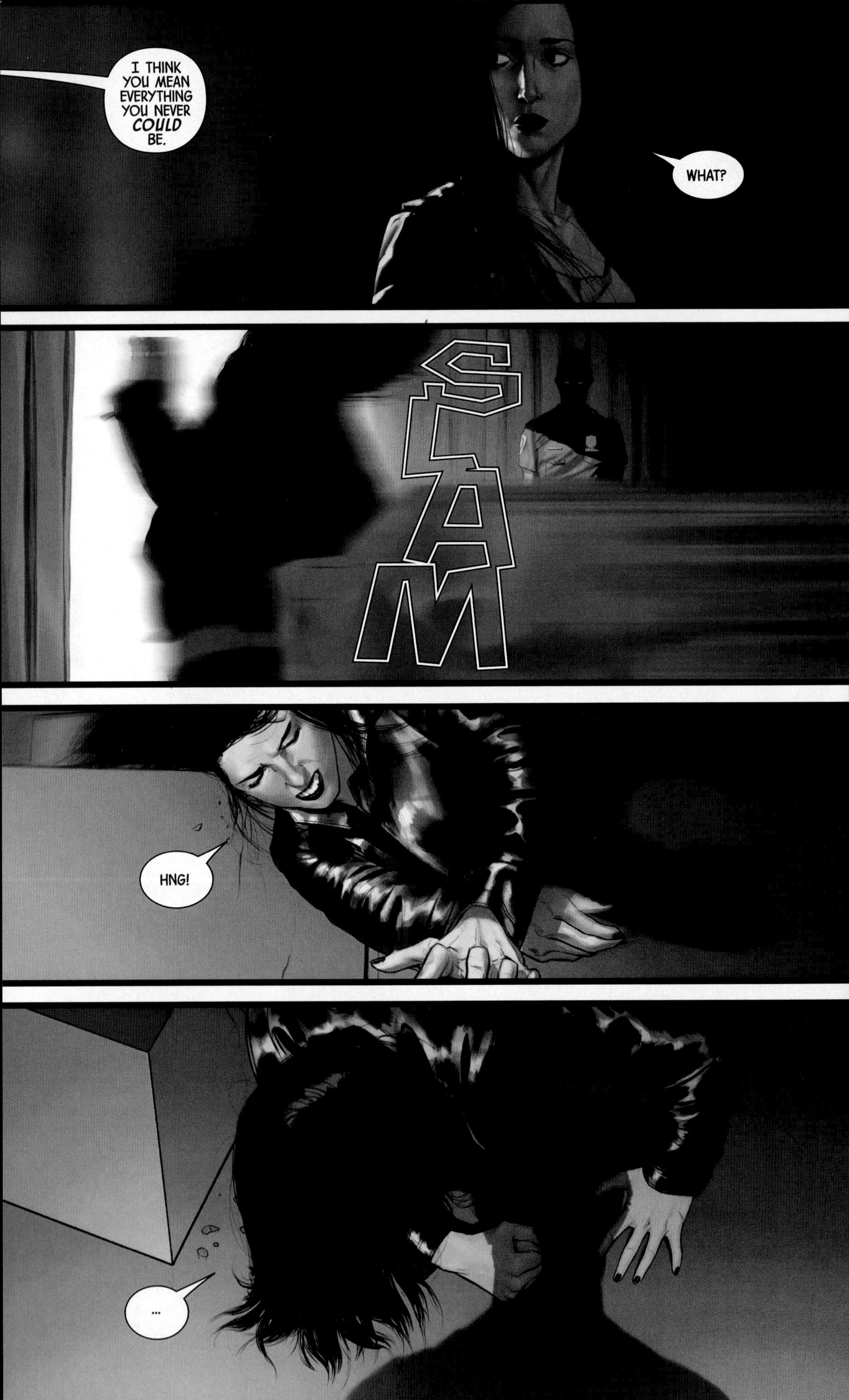
I THINK YOU MEAN EVERYTHING YOU NEVER COULD BE.
WHAT?
SLAM
HNG!
...

THAT FELT LIKE GETTING HIT BY A TRUCK.
YOU'LL NEVER UNDERSTAND. THEY NEVER DO.
WAIT... YOU?

TIME: NOW
LOCATION:
SOMEWHERE BAD
I CAN SEE IT ALL NOW, HOW ALL THE PIECES FIT, BUT LIVING LONG ENOUGH TO TELL THE TALE... THAT'S STILL A QUESTION MARK.

SO...IS THERE A GRAND PLAN HERE? BECAUSE SO FAR IT'S A LOT OF WAITING AROUND, AND I'M GETTING A LITTLE BORED.

AND WHILE WE'RE AT IT, WHY DOESN'T JARED HERE HAVE TO WEAR A COSTUME?

I MEAN, HERE I AM IN THE RIDICULOUS LIGHTNING BOLT SWIMSUIT, BUT HE'S JUST IN JEANS AND A T-SHIRT...HOW IS THAT FAIR? SEEMS A LITTLE SEXIST. BUT THAT'S NUTS, RIGHT?

I MEAN, YOU CLEARLY HAVE NO ISSUES WITH WOMEN. AT ALL.
I CAN'T WAIT TO KILL YOU ALL OVER AGAIN, LADY.
BAD JARED.
YEAH. SHOCKING.
GOOD JARED.

5

TIME: STILL NOW
LOCATION: STILL BAD
IF THERE'S ONE GOOD THING ABOUT BEING ME, IT'S THAT PEOPLE ALWAYS UNDERESTIMATE ME.
ON EVERY LEVEL.
INCLUDING LITERAL STRENGTH.

IT'S INSULTING... BUT Y'KNOW WHAT? I'LL TAKE IT. MAKES IT EASIER TO WIN.
HNNNGGGGAH!

...YOU COULD DO THAT THE WHOLE TIME?
YES.
UM...THEN WHY DID YOU WAIT SO LONG?

WELL, DIA'S POWERS, AND THUS BOTH YOURS AND "OTHER JARED'S," SEEM TO WARP REALITY.
SO IF I BREAK FREE IN FRONT OF HIM, THEN HE JUST CONJURES UP THICKER CHAINS...AND WHO KNOWS WHAT ELSE.
OH. YEAH. THAT MAKES SENSE.

ALTHOUGH...AS I'M STRUGGLING WITH THESE KNOTS, IT OCCURS TO ME THAT YOU CAN MAYBE JUST "REALITY WARP" YOUR WAY OUT OF THEM, NO?
I DON'T THINK SO...THE POWER... IT DOESN'T SEEM TO WORK THE SAME WAY FOR ME THAT IT DOES FOR HIM. I'M NOT IN CONTROL. THE ONLY THING THAT SEEMS TO WORK IS REVERSING BAD SHIT HE DOES.
THE FIRST TIME I DID IT, IT WAS AN ACCIDENT. SORT OF LIKE HOW IT WAS FOR DIA.
WHY ARE THE BAD GUYS ALWAYS BETTER AT WIELDING DEADLY WEAPONS? SO ANNOYING.
HOLY SHIT! DIA! YOU'RE ALIVE!
...HI, JARED.
HEY, DIA. I WONDERED IF YOU WERE HERE.
Y-YEAH... I...I DID THE INVISIBILITY THING.
I HOPED YOU WOULD. I'M REALLY PROUD OF YOU. YOU OKAY?
...I--I HAVE NEVER BEEN MORE FRIGHTENED IN MY LIFE.
WELCOME TO SUPER-POWERS.
THINK YOU CAN HELP ME WITH THESE ROPES?
NO! SHE HAS TO GET OUT OF HERE. SHE HAS TO GET AS FAR AWAY FROM HIM AS POSSIBLE. HE WON'T STOP UNTIL SHE'S DEAD. IT'S ALL HE CARES ABOUT.
EVERYTHING HE'S DONE IS ABOUT GETTING TO HER, KILLING HER.
I'M AWARE. BUT DIA IS A GOOD PERSON AND SHE'S NOT GOING TO LET EVIL JARED CONTINUE ON HIS KILLING-POWERFUL-WOMEN SPREE JUST SO SHE CAN HIDE OUT. WE GOTTA STOP HIM, RIGHT, DIA?
...YES.
THANK YOU.
SO, JARED, HOW THE HELL DID THIS ALL HAPPEN?
I AM SO SORRY, DIA. FOR EVERYTHING.

TIME: BEFORE
LOCATION: MANHATTAN
"I...WE...I WOKE UP ONE DAY WITH DIA'S POWER. BUT IT WAS HARD FOR ME TO CONTROL, JUST LIKE IT WAS FOR HER.
"AND I...I DIDN'T FEEL... IT DIDN'T MAKE ME FEEL HOW I THOUGHT IT WOULD...POWERFUL, IN CONTROL, BETTER.
"AND IT DIDN'T MAKE ME ANY LESS ANGRY.
"I HATED MYSELF SO MUCH.
"I WISHED...I WISHED I COULD GET RID OF EVERYTHING BAD ABOUT MYSELF...KEEP ONLY WHAT WAS GOOD...
Meatball
"I THINK...I THINK I WISHED IT REALLY HARD.

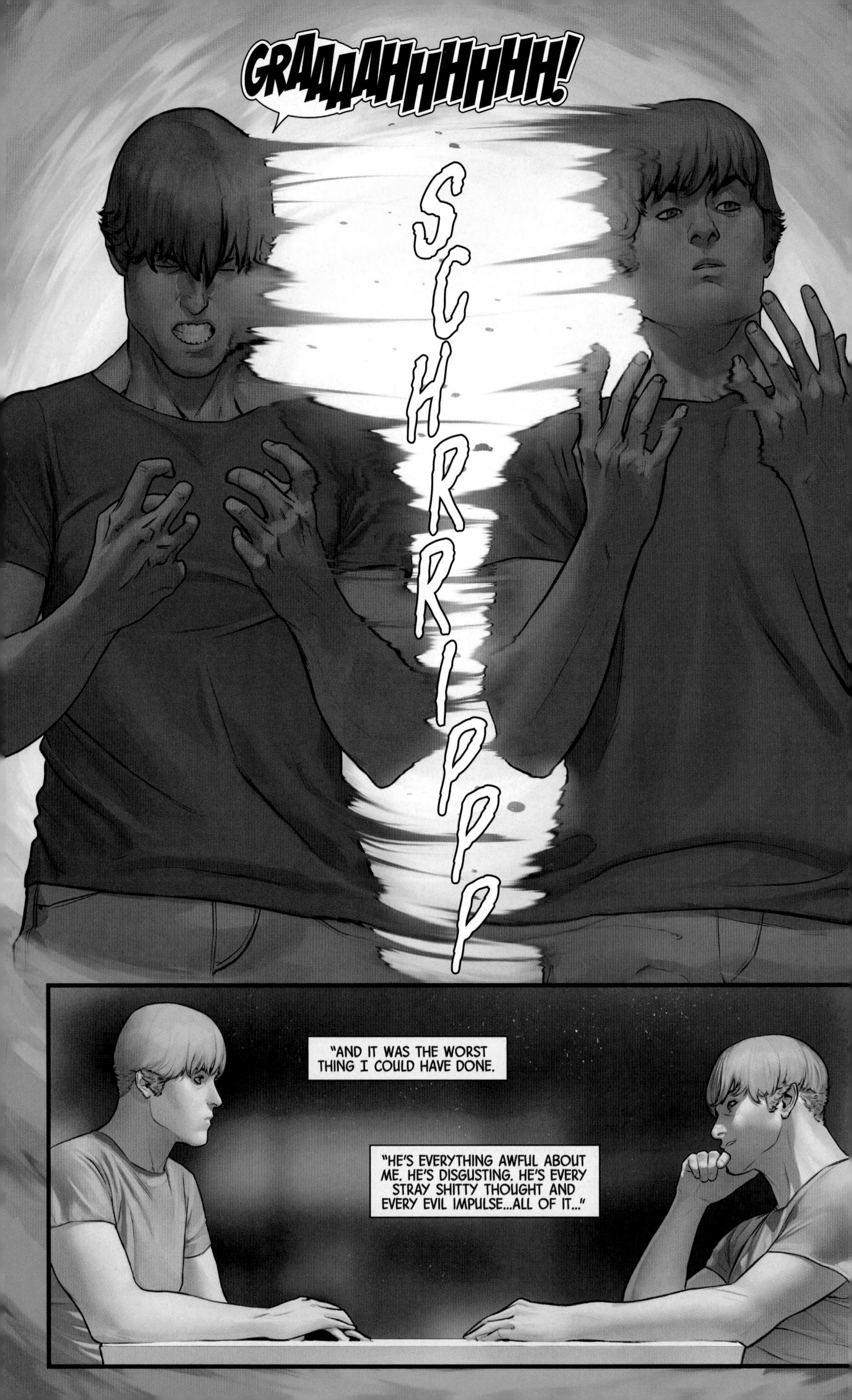
GRAAAAHHHHHH!
SCHRIPPP
"AND IT WAS THE WORST THING I COULD HAVE DONE.
"HE'S EVERYTHING AWFUL ABOUT ME. HE'S DISGUSTING. HE'S EVERY STRAY SHITTY THOUGHT AND EVERY EVIL IMPULSE...ALL OF IT..."

...AND ALL HE WANTS IS TO KILL YOU, DIA. I'M SO SORRY.
DIA LOOKS READY TO BOLT. HARD TO BLAME HER. THIS IS TEN KINDS OF MESSED UP.
...
OKAY. LET'S TAKE IT DOWN A COUPLE NOTCHES HERE.
JARED...IF THE EVIL YOU JUST WANTS TO KILL DIA, WHY IS HE KILLING THESE OTHER WOMEN?
SOME OF THEM ARE WOMEN LIKE YOU AND ELSA, WHO HE BELIEVED HELPED DIA, AND WHO HE THOUGHT SHOULD BE "PUT IN THEIR PLACE," AS FAR AS I CAN TELL.
OTHERS ARE JUST WOMEN WHO INSULTED HIM...US...OR GOT IN OUR WAY. LIKE SKEIN AND WHITE RABBIT AND EVEN MS. WATSON.
"PUT IN THEIR PLACE." *UGH.* NO REAL SURPRISE THERE.
SPEAKING OF SKEIN AND WHITE RABBIT...WHY DIDN'T YOU SAVE THEM?
I DIDN'T KNOW WHAT HE WAS DOING YET. I MEAN...WE'RE NOT THE SAME...IT'S NOT LIKE I KNOW WHAT HE'S THINKING. BUT WHEN I REALIZED HE MIGHT BE BEHIND WHAT HAPPENED TO SKEIN AND WHITE RABBIT, I STARTED FOLLOWING HIM...
...TRYING TO FIX WHAT HE BROKE.
DO YOU KNOW ***WHY*** HE WANTS TO KILL DIA SO BADLY? LIKE, IS THERE A REASON WE'RE MISSING BEYOND THE OBVIOUS FACT THAT HE'S A COMPLETE DICK WITH CONTROL ISSUES?
...NO. I--I DON'T KNOW.
YOU'RE GONNA HAVE TO GO DEEPER THAN THAT, JARED. I KNOW YOU DON'T LIKE BEING IN HIS HEAD, BUT YOU'RE OBVIOUSLY THE PERSON WHO KNOWS HIM BEST...HE ***WAS*** YOU AT ONE TIME.
EVEN THOUGH YOU ABHOR THOSE FEELINGS NOW, THEY WERE ONCE YOUR OWN. YOU'RE GONNA HAVE TO DIG DEEP AND GIVE US THAT EDGE WE DESPERATELY NEED.
IN THE MEANTIME...

OOM
LIKE I SAID. PEOPLE UNDERESTIMATING MY POWER IS A *WHOLE THING.*
AY NOT LOOK MUCH, BUT E ABOUT TO THE WORLD...
...OR AT LEAST A WHOLE LOT OF COOL BITCHES WHO DON'T KNOW THAT THIS GUY IS LURKING AROUND EVERY CORNER JUST WAITING TO KILL THEM IF HE DOESN'T LIKE THEIR SMILE.

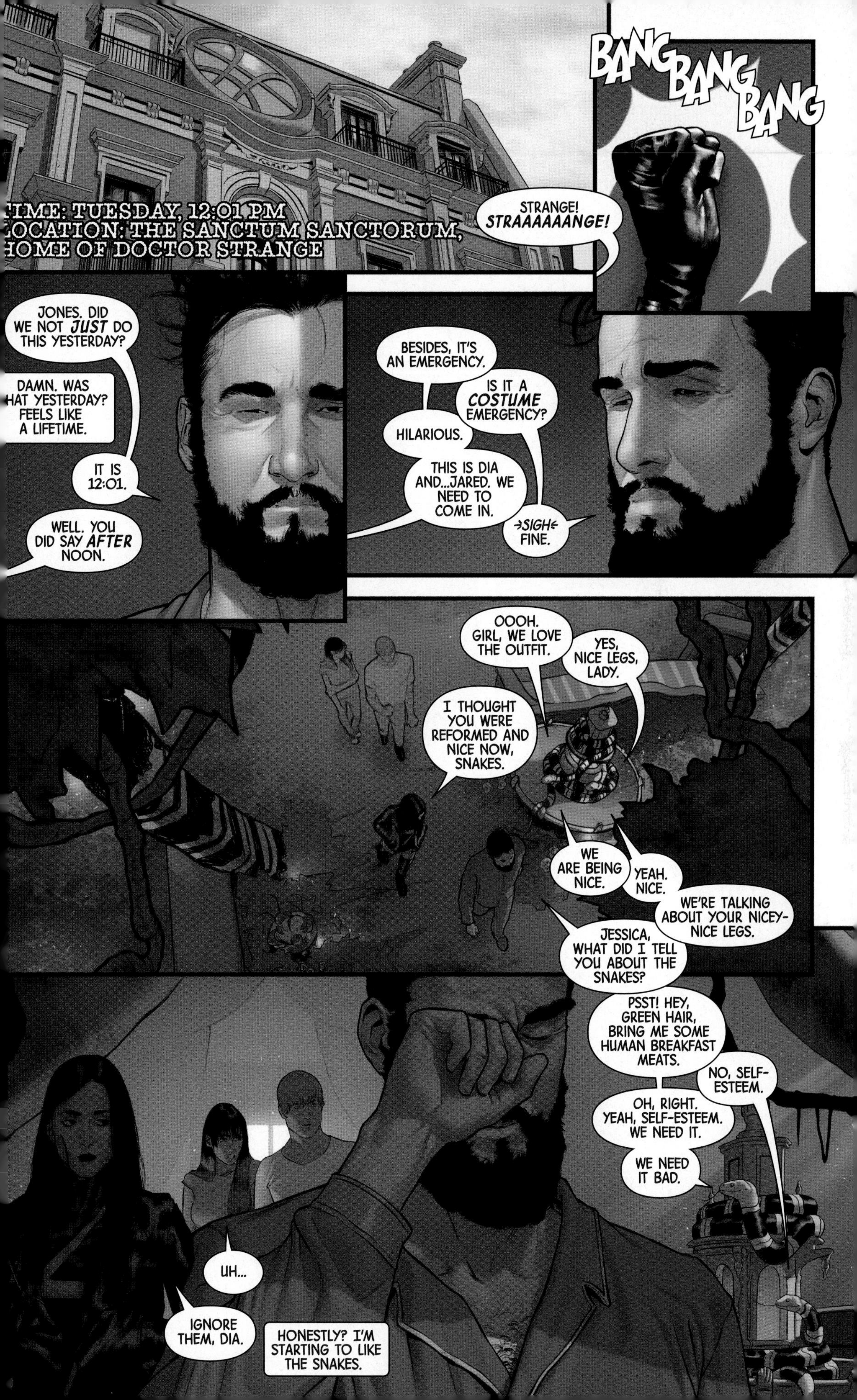

IME: TUESDAY, 12:01 PM
OCATION: THE SANCTUM SANCTORUM,
HOME OF DOCTOR STRANGE
BANG BANG BANG
STRANGE! STRAAAAAANGE!
JONES. DID WE NOT JUST DO THIS YESTERDAY?
DAMN. WAS HAT YESTERDAY? FEELS LIKE A LIFETIME.
IT IS 12:01.
WELL. YOU DID SAY AFTER NOON.
BESIDES, IT'S AN EMERGENCY.
IS IT A COSTUME EMERGENCY?
HILARIOUS.
THIS IS DIA AND...JARED. WE NEED TO COME IN.
SIGH FINE.
OOOH. GIRL, WE LOVE THE OUTFIT.
YES, NICE LEGS, LADY.
I THOUGHT YOU WERE REFORMED AND NICE NOW, SNAKES.
WE ARE BEING NICE.
YEAH. NICE.
WE'RE TALKING ABOUT YOUR NICEY-NICE LEGS.
JESSICA, WHAT DID I TELL YOU ABOUT THE SNAKES?
PSST! HEY, GREEN HAIR, BRING ME SOME HUMAN BREAKFAST MEATS.
NO, SELF-ESTEEM.
OH, RIGHT. YEAH, SELF-ESTEEM. WE NEED IT.
WE NEED IT BAD.
UH...
IGNORE THEM, DIA.
HONESTLY? I'M STARTING TO LIKE THE SNAKES.

SO. WHAT PETTY LITTLE THING ARE WE BOTHERING ME WITH TODAY?
I AM QUITE BUSY, AS YOU CAN PERHAPS IMAGINE.
JUST GONNA IGNORE THAT ONE.
I SUPPOSE YOU COULD SAY I'VE GOT A REALITY-WARPER PROBLEM.
YOUR LITTLE FRIEND HERE? YES, I RECOGNIZE HER.
FROM WHERE?
WHEN YOU CAME BY YESTERDAY, I SAW HER ENERGY. LIKE SHE LEFT A MAGICAL FINGERPRINT ON YOU.
OKAY, WELL, DIA CAME BY THE POWER NATURALLY, BUT JARED SORT OF...INHERITED IT FROM HER.
INHERITED? OH, SHE GAVE IT TO HIM WITH HER *OWN* POWER... INTRIGUING.
THEN JARED WISHED THAT HE COULD EXCISE ALL THE BAD IN HIM AND ENDED UP SPLITTING HIMSELF IN TWO...
FASCINATING.
BECAUSE WE CERTAINLY NEEDED ANOTHER ONE OF THOSE.
YES. WELL, AS YOU CAN PROBABLY IMAGINE, JAMMING ALL THE CRAPPY PARTS OF HIM OFF INTO ONE PERSON HAS CREATED A VILLAIN... WITH REALITY-WARPING POWERS.
EXACTLY. SO I'M TRYING TO TAKE CARE OF IT. AND I NEED YOUR HELP...OR RATHER, *THEY* NEED YOUR HELP. THEY NEED TRAINING. THEY NEED TO BETTER UNDERSTAND HOW TO CONTROL THEIR POWERS.
SO THEY DON'T END UP WITH TEN-INCH FOREHEADS... OR SPLIT INTO JEKYLL AND HYDES.

TEN-INCH FOREHEADS?

IT'S A THING... OR MAYBE JUST A METAPHOR...OR, I DON'T KNOW. LISTEN, THE POINT IS, DO YOU WANT TO HELP BEFORE THE BIG BAD REALITY WARPER LEVELS UP OR NOT?
LET'S GET IN ON THE GROUND FLOOR OF THIS ONE, STRANGE. BEFORE HE GROWS TENTACLES AND SHIT.

I ***DO*** HATE TENTACLES.
WHO DOESN'T?

BEEP
WHO ARE YOU CALLING?
A FRIEND.
YOU'RE LEAVING, AREN'T YOU? I DON'T WANT YOU TO LEAVE. WHAT IF EVIL JARED FINDS US?
HE WON'T. AND IF HE DOES, THIS PLACE IS LIKE A FORTRESS. PLUS, I'VE CALLED IN SOME REINFORCEMENTS.
YOU REMEMBER ELSA BLOODSTONE?

DIA, I DON'T WANT TO FREAK YOU OUT, BUT THIS IS GOING TO COME DOWN TO YOU. I MAY BE HARD TO KILL, BUT SUPER-POWERED PUNCHES ARE NO MATCH FOR SOMEONE WHO CAN BEND REALITY TO THEIR WILL.
WHY? WHY CAN'T MR. STRANGE DO IT? WHY CAN'T WE CALL THE AVENGERS?
I KNOW FROM VERY PAINFUL PERSONAL EXPERIENCE THAT WHEN YOU HAVE A DEMON LIKE JARED IN YOUR LIFE, YOU HAVE TO DEAL WITH IT YOURSELF OR YOU'LL ALWAYS BE RUNNING.
DOESN'T MEAN YOU CAN'T HAVE HELP, BUT AT THE END OF THE DAY, THE ONLY WAY YOU'LL BE ABLE TO MOVE ON IS IF YOU TAKE RESPONSIBILITY... AND STAND UP.
YOU'RE STRONGER THAN HE IS, AND I NEED YOU TO ***KNOW*** THAT, DIA. I NEED YOU TO ***OWN*** IT.
...
OR WE'RE GONNA GET CREAMED.

DIDN'T THINK I'D BE BABYSITTING ON MY OWN, JONES. YOU'RE GONNA OWE ME WHEN THIS IS ALL OVER.
HEY. HEY, RED! LOOKIT THEM LEGS...THEY GO ALL THE WAY UP!
I THINK YOU'RE A LEG MAN...ER, LEG SNAKE.
YES. I THINK SO TOO.
YOU SAY ANOTHER NASTY THING LIKE THAT TO ME AGAIN, SNAKES, AND I'M GONNA TIE YOUR SODDING TAILS TOGETHER AND ☠☠☠☠ ☠☠☠☠ ☠☠☠☠ ☠☠☠☠.
OH MY.
...I THINK I'M IN LOVE.
IF YOU DON'T MIND, MS. BLOODSTONE, THIS REQUIRES RATHER A GREAT DEAL OF CONCENTRATION.
YOUR BLOODY SNAKES STARTED IT.
I HAVE NO DOUBT. PLEASE TRY TO RESIST STOOPING TO THEIR LEVEL.
PFFT. LEVEL. I'LL SHOW YOU A ☠☠☠☠☠ LEVEL.
THIS IS SOME FAVOR, JONES. WHATEVER YOU'RE PLANNING HAD BETTER BLOODY BE WORTH IT.
VERY GOOD, DIA. CAN YOU SEE HOW IT IS SIMULTANEOUSLY ABOUT FOCUS AND WILL? YOU HAVE TO HAVE THE WILL TO MAKE IT REALITY, BUT WITHOUT THE CLARITY OF MIND TO FOCUS IT, IT BECOMES A MESS.
YES...YES, I'M BEGINNING TO SEE.
I'M NOT. CAN'T YOU JUST MAGIC US INTO UNDERSTANDING HOW TO CONTROL THIS STUFF LIKE IN THE MOVIES OR SOMETHING?
→SIGH← I HATE MOVIES.
...I SEE.

TIME: TUESDAY, 7:07 PM
LOCATION:
EAST RIVER PARK
PROMENADE
SCREEEEEECH
HANDS IN THE AIR!
YOU'RE UNDER ARREST.
THIS...ISN'T EXACTLY WHAT I HAD IN MIND WHEN I CALLED YOU, AGENT KNIGHT...
WELL, YOU SAID IT WAS BIG, I THOUGHT...BIG DESERVES BIG.
DIA SLOANE. YOU'RE UNDER ARREST...FOR STARTERS. WE'LL SEE WHAT ELSE AFTER WE PUT YOU IN THE BOX.
YOU SHOULD GET THESE PEOPLE CLEAR. THIS IS GOING TO GO BAD FAST.
YOU LET ME WORRY ABOUT THAT, MISS SLOANE.
JESSICA TOLD ME YOU WERE ANNOYING.
YES, WELL, TAKES ONE TO KNOW ONE, I SUPPOSE.

YOU'VE BEEN VERY, VERY CLEVER IN HOW YOU'VE BEEN HIDING FROM ME...
...BUT YOU SHOULD HAVE KNOWN I'D NEVER STOP LOOKING FOR YOU, DIA...
THEN I'M AFRAID I'VE GOT BAD NEWS...

...YOU'VE STILL GOT SOME LOOKING TO DO, SON.
BOOM
KR-KRASH

JUST STAY OWN, JARED. OUR LIFE AS A UPER VILLAIN IS OVER.
ON THE CONTRARY, MS. JONES. IT'S JUST BEGINNING.
HNG.
FWOOOOSH
BOOM

MS. JONES. I ALREADY KILLED YOU ONCE. YOU'D THINK YOU WOULD LEARN.
THOUGH I'M IMPRESSED YOU'RE STILL IN THE COSTUME... PERHAPS YOU DOTH PROTEST TOO MUCH ON THAT FRONT, HUH?
OR PERHAPS I JUST WANTED THE WORLD TO SEE YOU GET THE *CRAP* KICKED OUT OF YOU BY A *WOMAN IN A SWIMSUIT.*
AND ONE IN *STILETTOS.*
OOOOOOOF!
FOOOMP
THAT'S FOR SHOOTING ME IN THE BACK OF THE HEAD LIKE A PISSY, COWARDLY LITTLE ☠☠☠☠!
POW

YOU ALL RIGHT, JONES?
BEEN BETTER. HIT HIM HARDER, PLEASE.
AS YOU WISH, DARLING.
POW

STUPID BITCHES DON'T KNOW WHEN TO STAY DOWN.
BLOODY HELL.
FWOOOOSH
BUT IF YOU WON'T STAY DOWN, HOW ABOUT YOU STAY DROWN?
SPLASH
YOUR WITTY BANTER NEEDS SERIOUS WORK, KID.
IMAGINE MY COMPLETE LACK OF CONCERN.
NEVER SHOULD HAVE USED A BULLET ON YOU ANYWAY. TOO QUICK, TOO EASY. I SHOULD HAVE MADE YOU SUFFER. I SHOULD HAVE ENJOYED IT MORE.
→HRK← GUYS LIKE YOU ALWAYS →HRK← SEEM TO HAVE A PROBLEM WITH →HRK← SPEED.
JOKING. EVEN NOW. PATHETIC.

YOU TRYING TO SAY SOMETHING? MAKE IT GOOD, JONES, THOSE WORDS WILL BE YOUR LAST.
→HRKKK← YOU FEELING →HRRK← OKAY? DON'T →HRK← LOOK SO GOOD.
WHAT ARE YOU... WAIT...I...
NO...WHAT-- WHAT HAVE YOU DONE?!
NOT ME, BIG BOY. →KOFF← DIA.
SEE...WE ALL THOUGHT IT WAS JUST YOUR EXTREMELY DISTURBING OBSESSION WITH HER THAT WAS DRIVING YOU SO HARD TO TRY TO FIND HER. →KOFF← BUT DIA FIGURED IT OUT.
SHE REALIZED WHAT YOU ALREADY KNEW...THAT BECAUSE SHE GAVE YOU YOUR POWER, SHE COULD ALSO...
...TAKE IT ALL AWAY.
HELL YES.
NO.

ARED, IT'S YOUR TURN. KE WE TALKED ABOUT... YOU NEED TO REABSORB HIM.
I...I DON'T WANT TO. I DON'T WANT ALL THAT HORRIBLE SHIT BACK INSIDE ME. JUST LOOK AT HIM--WHY DO WE WANT ME TO TAKE THAT BACK?
I KNOW YOU DON'T WANT TO, BUT YOU HAVE TO.
WHY?! IF YOU COULD JETTISON EVERYTHING HORRIBLE ABOUT YOURSELF, WOULDN'T YOU?
HELL YES.
WOULD YOU TAKE IT BACK?
NOT A CHANCE.
HERE'S THE THING...THAT'S TEMPTING AS HELL. ANYONE WOULD WANT THAT. BUT THAT'S NOT THE WAY THE WORLD WORKS. THERE IS NO MAGICAL OUT...YOU CAN'T MAGIC YOURSELF INTO BEING A BETTER PERSON.
EXCEPT YOU CAN! IT'S HAPPENED! I DID IT!
BUT YOU DIDN'T LEARN ANYTHING, JARED.
YOU REMOVED THE SHIT THAT WAS TOXIC, BUT YOU DIDN'T LEARN WHY IT WAS TOXIC. YOU DIDN'T DO THE HARD WORK TO MAKE SURE THAT YOU WOULDN'T DO IT ALL AGAIN.
BUT...IT DOESN'T HAVE TO BE THAT WAY.
SO HERE'S A THING I'M GOING TO SAY, AND IT'S CLICHÉ AS HELL, BUT IT'S A CLICHÉ FOR A REASON... THOSE WHO DON'T LEARN FROM HISTORY ARE DOOMED TO REPEAT IT. THERE'S A GOOD CHANCE YOU'LL JUST BECOME HIM ALL OVER AGAIN ANYWAY.
...
AND EVEN IF I WAS WRONG ABOUT ALL THAT OTHER STUFF--
I'M NOT.
--BUT EVEN IF I WAS, I THINK WE ALL KNOW HOW MUCH DAMAGE A BAD MAN CAN DO TO THE WORLD, EVEN WITHOUT SUPER-POWERS. WE SEE IT EVERY DAY. HE CAN'T BE ALLOWED TO JUST EXIST LIKE THIS.
YOU HAVE TO TAKE HIM BACK INTO YOU AND ACCEPT THAT ALL THAT SHIT IS PART OF YOU, OR AT LEAST YOUR PAST, AND YOU HAVE TO LEARN TO BE BETTER. IT'S THE ONLY WAY.

NO. *NO.* YOU CAN'T DO THIS. SHE'S LYING TO YOU!
NO. I WISH SHE WAS. BUT SHE'S REALLY NOT.
NOOOO!
GUH.

SO--YOU'LL NEVER GUESS WHO MISTY SAID WOKE UP IN THE MORGUE.
☠☠☠! NO.
YUP. SKEIN AND WHITE RABBIT.
COULD BE. REALITY WARPING IS NOTHING IF NOT COMPLEX.
WOW. YOU THINK BY ABSORBING EVIL JARED, WE UNDID HIS CRIMES?
WHAT WILL HAPPEN TO JARED NOW?
I DON'T KNOW. THE CIRCUMSTANCES ARE OBVIOUSLY COMPLICATED, BUT HE SAVED LIVES, AND THAT WON'T GO UNNOTICED. PLUS, THERE AREN'T ACTUALLY ANY MURDER CHARGES TO FILE NOW...SO THAT'LL BE INTERESTING.
YOU OWE ME ONE, JONES.
I THOUGHT WE WERE EVEN.
NOT AT ALL. YOU OWE ME.
DAMN. SHE STRIKES ME AS SOMEONE WHO ALWAYS COLLECTS.
AND YOU, DIA, DARLING...I'M GLAD YOU'RE ALIVE. DON'T EVER BLOODY COME NEAR ME AGAIN.
WHAT WILL YOU DO NOW?
I THINK I'LL GO BACK UPSTATE. IT WAS CALMER THERE AND I NEED THAT. BUT DR. STRANGE HAS OFFERED TO CONTINUE MY MEDITATION TRAINING ONCE A WEEK IN THE CITY.
GOOD. I LIKE THIS PLAN FOR YOU.
JESSICA...I WANTED TO SAY, WELL, "THANK YOU" DOESN'T SEEM ENOUGH, BUT... THANK YOU.
I'M NOT SURE WHAT YOU'RE THANKING ME FOR. I LET YOU DOWN ALL THOSE YEARS AGO AND THEN DRAGGED YOU THROUGH YOUR OWN PERSONAL HELL--ALL YOUR WORST FEARS REALIZED.
WELL. I GUESS IN THE END, IT'S THE SAME FOR ME AS IT IS FOR JARED.
I COULDN'T JUST KEEP RUNNING... I HAD TO LEARN, I HAD TO GROW. WHAT ELSE IS THERE IF NOT THAT? YOU SAVED ME. IT WASN'T WHAT I THOUGHT I NEEDED, BUT IS IT EVER?
AREN'T WE THE WORST AT KNOWING WHAT WE NEED?
WELL, THAT HIT TOO CLOSE TO HOME.
...YOU'RE WELCOME. NOW GO GET YOUR CAT BACK.

TIME: TUESDAY, 9:22 PM

DIA SLOANE'S CASE, FINALLY CLOSED. I FAILED HER ALL THOSE YEARS AGO, AND EVER SINCE THEN, HER CASE HAS BEEN LIKE A PEBBLE IN MY SHOE.
SURE, I HAD TO GET SHOT IN THE HEAD--AMONG OTHER THINGS--TO GET THE PEBBLE OUT OF SAID METAPHORICAL SHOE, BUT IT ALL WORKED OUT IN THE END.

THIS ALL BEGAN WITH BLIND SPOTS. BLIND SPOTS BEING BAD SURPRISES. BUT MAYBE THAT'S NAIVE.

MAYBE A BAD THING ONLY LOOKS LIKE A BAD THING FROM A CERTAIN ANGLE. MAYBE FROM ANOTHER ANGLE IT'S SOMETHING ELSE ENTIRELY.

DIA SLOANE

CASE IN POINT. WAS THERE EVER A BIGGER BLIND SPOT IN MY LIFE THAN LUKE FREAKING CAGE? OR OUR DAUGHTER, DANI?

LUKE CAGE...WHY ISN'T MY BABY IN BED ALREADY?

OH, THE SLEEP SCHEDULE WAS THE FIRST THING TO GO.
DO YOU SAY OUT LOUD HOW MUCH YOU MISS THEM TOO? IS THAT JUST ASKING FOR THINGS TO BE TORN APART AGAIN?
I SAW THE NEWS. WE MISSED YOU.
MAYBE IF YOU PRETEND YOU CARE LESS, THE WORLD WON'T NOTICE THAT IT GAVE YOU SOMETHING TO LOVE.
MAYBE THEN IT WON'T TRY TO TAKE IT FROM YOU.

...I MISSED YOU TOO.

SHOULD WE TALK ABOUT THE OUTFIT? I FEEL LIKE WE SHOULD TALK ABOUT THE OUTFIT. OR AT LEAST BRING IT HOME WITH US.
SCREW IT. I'M GONNA BET THE FARM ON A GOOD SURPRISE.

OH, IT'S COMING HOME WITH US.

6
HAPPY BIRTHDAY

TIME:
SATURDAY, 8:03 AM
LOCATION: HARLEM
HOME OF
JESSICA JONES,
LUKE CAGE AND
DANIELLE CAGE

...
IT'S AFTER EIGHT!

DON'T KNOW WHY DANI DIDN'T WAKE US UP, BUT SHE PICKED A HELL OF A DAY TO SLEEP IN AND--
WHAT? MY TURN!
NO FAIR!

...WHO IS SHE TALKING TO?
'S JUS' THE TV, JESS.
THE TV DOESN'T ANSWER BACK.

LUKE. GET THE HELL UP.
I'M GETTING, I'M GETTING.

YAAAAAAA

AAAA? JEN?
MFFFF. HEYFF, JESFFF.
MOMMA! HULK!
I SEE HER, HONEY.
JEN, WHAT ARE YOU DOING HERE? YOU SCARED ME HALF TO DEATH.
SORRY. EATING.
YES, I CAN SEE THAT. AND THANK YOU FOR FEEDING MY DAUGHTER CUPCAKES FOR BREAKFA-- WAIT--ARE THOSE HER BIRTHDAY PARTY CUPCAKES YOU'RE EATING?
SORRY?

JEN, WHAT THE HELL? HOW DID YOU EVEN GET IN HERE?
MFFFT. WINDOW.

GREAT.

JEN, WHY ARE YOU HERE AT EIGHT IN THE MORNING?
PRESENT.
YAAAAY!

THAT'S VERY SWEET, JEN, BUT THE PARTY ISN'T UNTIL THIS AFTERNOON. YOU COULDN'T HAVE WAITED?
BUSY LATER!
KRRRAK

LUKE! C'MON!
→SIGH←
WHAT? WE'RE GONNA HAVE TO REPLACE THEM ANYWAY, RIGHT?
OOOOOH!
MAGIC TOY. MAKE DANI STRONG.
WAIT, NOT REALLY?
NO. NOT REALLY.
DON'T RUIN!

BYE, HULKIE!
HONEY, STOP SQUIRMING. NANNY PAM IS GOING TO BE HERE ANY MINUTE TO PICK YOU UP AND YOU STILL NEED TO GET DRESSED.

JEN! JUST USE THE FRONT DOO--
--ANNNNND SHE ALREADY JUMPED. TODAY IS GOING SO AWESOME.

BZZZZZZZZ
THAT'S NANNY...GO GET YOUR SHOES, BABY.
BZZZZZZ

SO, JEN JUST SAW *EVERYTHING* I GOT, BABE.
WELL, NO WONDER SHE JUMPED.

HOW DARE YOU, JONES.
IMPOSSIBLE.
YES, WELL, SOMEONE'S GOT TO KEEP YOUR MASSIVE EGO IN CHECK.
I JUST SAW SHE-HULK ALMOST LAND ON A GUY. IT WAS *AWESOME.*

NO MORE SUGAR FOR HER TODAY, PAM. SHE HAD CUPCAKES FOR BREAKFAST AND OF COURSE THERE WILL BE MORE SWEETS LATER.
SWEETS!
NO PROBLEM.
YOU WANT US BACK AROUND THREE O'CLOCK, RIGHT?
THAT WOULD BE PERFECT.

HOW CAN IT ONLY BE 8:15?
AT LEAST THEY'RE GOOD ONES.
I HAVE NO IDEA. I STILL DON'T EVEN HAVE ANY PANTS ON. PAM SAW MY UNDERWEAR.
MAYBE. IF EVERYTHING TODAY GOES RIGHT.
WE GOTTA GET NEW CUPCAKES. IF I CALL, DO YOU THINK YOU COULD PICK THEM UP?
WHY ARE WE DOING THIS AGAIN?
HA. THAT'S HILARIOUS.
BECAUSE DANI INSISTED ON TURNING TWO.
HOW MANY MORE BIRTHDAYS WILL THERE BE?
LIKE...A THOUSAND? IF WE'RE LUCKY?
WHERE ARE THE DECORATIONS YOU BOUGHT?
HALL CLOSET.

HI, BLAINE. YEAH, JESSICA JONES. UH-HUH.
WELL, THE CUPCAKES *WERE* DELICIOUS, BUT UNFORTUNATELY, I NEED MORE. LOTS MORE. TODAY.
UH-HUH. OKAY. "HAPPY BIRTHDAY DANIELLE" ON IT? GREAT.
THANKS SO MUCH.
WHAT HAPPENED?
HE CAN'T DO ANYTHING CUSTOM, BUT HE'S GOT A CAKE THAT WILL WORK. HE'S PUTTING HER NAME ON IT. READY IN TEN.
HONESTLY, IT'S MAYBE GOOD THAT JEN ISN'T GOING TO BE HERE LATER--I'M STILL NOT SURE HOW EVERYONE IS GONNA FIT IN THIS APARTMENT.

TRUE. MAYBE WE SHOULD DO IT SOMEWHERE ELSE?
I'M GOING TO PRETEND YOU DIDN'T SAY...

...
IT'S FINE.
DON'T SAY ANYTHING.
IT'S FINE. YOU'RE FINE.

WHAT'S WRONG? YOU SAID MERMAIDS AND UNICORNS.
...YEAH.
KNOCK KNOCK

YOU EXPECTING SOMEONE?
NO. YOU?
NO.

HAPPY BIRTHDAY, SMALLEST OF CAGES!
EXCELLENT FACE.
EXCELLENT ABS.
EXCELLENT... EVERYTHING.

DUDE. WHAT ARE YOU DOING HERE? IT'S NOT EVEN 8:30.

I WAS IN THY NEIGHBORHOOD?
LET ME GUESS, YOU CAME EARLY BECAUSE YOU'RE BUSY LATER.
NO?

THINE "EVITE" WAS CONFUSING. PERHAPS THOU SHOULDST HAVE ENLISTED A CALLIGRAPHER AND HAD INVITATIONS DELIVERED BY WONDROUS BIRDS OF PREY...OR DOVES.
DOVES WOULD HAVE BEEN NICE.
WELL, YOU'RE HERE NOW, BUDDY, THERE'S LOTS TO DO.
I SHALL RETURN--
NOPE. HOW 'BOUT YOU HANG SOME STREAMERS?
STREAMERS?

HOLD!
HOW DIDST THOU GET THIS?
JEN BROUGHT IT AS A GIFT FOR DANI.

DOST THOU WISH HER TO SUMMON TRICKSTER GODS AT SUCH A TENDER AGE?
UH...NO.
THEN I SHALL RETURN IT TO WHERE IT BELONGS.
REMIND ME TO KILL JENNIFER.
DONE.

YOU KNOW WHAT? CAN YOU DO US A FAVOR AND PICK UP THE CAKE?
CAKE? SURELY THERE IS SOMETHING FAR MORE PRESSING... SOMETHING WORTHY OF THOR.
I CONFESS INTRIGUE AT THESE "STREAMERS" THOU MENTIONED.
RIGHT. WELL, PLENTY OF TIME FOR THOSE AFTER YOU GET THE CAKE.

WHY ARE OUR FRIENDS LIKE THIS?
I DON'T KNOW, BUT I'M AFRAID OF WHAT IT SAYS ABOUT US.

NOW THOR SAW ME WITHOUT PANTS. JESUS. THIS DAY CAN JUST GO RIGHT TO HELL.

I FEEL LIKE MAYBE THIS WOULD GO EASIER IF YOU HELPED ME DO *THIS* AND THEN I COULD HELP YOU DO *THAT.*
...
NO. I'D PREFER TO NOT.

WELL, ALL RIGHT THEN. GREAT TALK.
KNOCK KNOCK

THAT WAS FA--

BOOM

WHO THE HELL...?
THE TWO OF YOU THINK YOU CAN SEND SOMEONE TO PRISON AND JUST NOT PAY FOR THAT? OH, YOU'RE GOING TO PAY!
THERE'S A SHARK.
A BIG ONE.
A SHARK IN MY GODDAMN HOME.
LONE SHARK. WE FOUGHT HIM ONCE BEFORE...WELL, MOSTLY LUKE. DANI WAS JUST A BABY. I THOUGHT HE WAS BEHIND BARS.

JAIL DOESN'T LAST AS LONG AS IT USED TO, I GUESS.
THIS IS OUR HOME. YOU'RE GONNA WANT TO GET OUT OF HERE RIGHT NOW.
OR YOU'LL BE LUCKY TO GO BACK TO PRISON, INSTEAD OF THE MORGUE.

PLEASE. NEITHER OF YOU ARE KILLERS... UNLIKE ME.

YOU FIRST, CAGE.

USUALLY IT'S →HRK← "LADIES FIRST," BUT OKAY.

LONE SHARK DOESN'T FOLLOW THE RULES!

OOF!
SLAM
CRASH

YOU GUYS HAVING THE PARTY ALREADY?
YIP! YIP!
MR. BENDOS, PLEASE GET OUT OF HERE!

BOOM

CRASH
BANG

WHAT'S UP WITH THE NAME, ANYWAY? "LOAN SHARK"? DOES SOMEONE OWE YOU MONEY? I DON'T GET IT.
IT...IT'S NOT "LOAN," IT'S "LONE," LIKE "LONE WOLF."

WELL, THAT'S DUMB. YOU KNOW NOBODY GETS THAT, RIGHT?
OH, 'CAUSE "POWER MAN" IS SO GOOD? YOU'RE DUMB!

BAM

BUT, MAN, A "LONE SHARK" ISN'T A THING. A "LONE WOLF" IS A THING. MAYBE YOU SHOULD CHANGE YOUR NAME TO LONE WOLF.
LUKE. CUT OUT THE WITTY BANTER AND JUST END THIS.

I'M A SHARK! I LIKE SHARKS!
FWOOOOOOOM

BOOOOOOOOOOOOM

I DON'T KNOW WHAT KIND OF MORON YOU HAVE TO BE TO ATTACK PARENTS OF A SMALL CHILD IN THEIR OWN HOME, BUT I'M ABOUT TO GO EXTREME VENGEANCE ON YOU, ASSHOLE.
KICK

WELCOME TO MY WORLD, JONES.

I DON'T WANT TO KILL THIS GUY ON MY KID'S BIRTHDAY.
PLUS, THAT WILL MAKE AN EVEN BIGGER MESS.
FWOMP
OOOOF!

KA-POW!

JUS-JUST GIMME A SECOND HERE...
NO.
BOOM
SMASH
WAIT...ARE YOU...ARE YOU TRYING TO THROW A BIRTHDAY PARTY FOR YOUR KID?
YES, YOU IDIOT.

OH MAN. I...I'M SORRY.
Y'KNOW, I WAITED UNTIL THE NANNY TOOK THE KID 'CAUSE I DIDN'T WANT TO ATTACK YOU WHEN SHE WAS AROUND, BUT I DIDN'T KNOW, Y'KNOW...
...IT'S A REAL JERK THAT RUINS A KID'S BIRTHDAY PARTY.
NO KIDDING.
HEY. I DIDN'T KNOW, OKAY?

YOU WANT TO JUST LET HIM GO?
I SO DON'T EVEN GIVE A SHIT.

I DON'T THINK WE SHOULD BE JUST LETTING HIM GO.
FINE. SO CALL THE COPS. I'VE GOT TOO MUCH OTHER CRAP TO DO, LUKE.

JESS, WHAT'S GOING ON?
YOU MEAN OTHER THAN WE JUST HAD TO FIGHT A DUMB, SHARK-BASED SUPER VILLAIN IN OUR APARTMENT AND IT GOT ALL WRECKED... *AGAIN?*
YES. OTHER THAN THAT...WHAT'S HAPPENING?

JESS, TALK TO ME.
I DON'T WANT TO TALK RIGHT NOW, LUKE.

OH. OH GOD. IT'S *HIM.*

"KILLGRAVE. THE PURPLE MAN. I'M SO DUMB."

IT'S THE *PURPLE.* THE *DECORATIONS.* YOU'RE HAVING SOME SORT OF PTSD REACTION TO THESE DUMB PURPLE DECORATIONS I BOUGHT.
WHAT? NO.

JESS, YOU'VE BEEN ON EDGE SINCE THE SECOND YOU *SAW* THE DECORATIONS...I BOUGHT *PURPLE.* AND THAT...THAT WAS SO DUMB. YOU HAVE BEEN DEEPLY AND PERMANENTLY TRAUMATIZED BY A MAN LITERALLY CALLED *THE PURPLE MAN.*
YOU *HATE* THIS COLOR. AND THERE I GO DRENCHING THE APARTMENT IN IT. I WASN'T THINKING.
AND I AM SO SORRY.

NO. C'MON, THAT'S NOT IT. THAT'S ABSURD. I--I DON'T GET UPSET ABOUT A FREAKING *COLOR.* THAT'S RIDICULOUS.

NO, IT'S NOT. IT MAKES ALL THE SENSE IN THE WORLD. AND I'M SO SORRY I DIDN'T SEE IT.
I...
JESSIE. IT'S OKAY. YOU CAN BE WEAK HERE...YOU CAN BE EMOTIONAL...
...YOU CAN BE VULNERABLE. I'M THE PERSON YOU CAN BE THAT WITH. STOP TRYING TO BE SO STRONG ALL THE DAMN TIME...STOP TRYING TO BE "FINE."
IT'S *OKAY* TO NOT BE FINE.

OKAY.

...

DOVES COULD HAVE SOLVED ALL OF THIS.
CERTAINLY THEY'LL NOT BEGRUDGE ME A BIT FROM THE END.

TIME: SATURDAY, 12:41 PM
--NOTICED SHE'S VERY CONCERNED WITH MERMAID PHYSIOLOGY.
YOU'RE TELLING ME. DO YOU KNOW HOW MERMAIDS GO POOP WITHOUT A BUTT? BECAUSE I DON'T, AND SHE IS NOT LETTING *THAT* QUESTION GO ANYTIME SOON.

IT'S GROSS, SURE, BUT DO YOU THINK IT'S *WEIRD?*
I MEAN, I THINK IT'S WEIRD THAT YOU'RE NOT MORE CONCERNED WITH IT BEING *GROSS*.
DON'T JUDGE ME!

THOR *ATE* SOME OF THIS! I CAN'T BELIEVE HE ATE THE CORNER OF MY DAUGHTER'S CAKE! UNBELIEVABLE!
I'M SHOCKED THAT YOU'RE SHOCKED.
JESSICA...LUKE? I...I KNOW WE'RE EARLY BUT...SOMETHING... SOMETHING'S HAPPENED.

D-DANI?
...

TO BE CONTINUED...

Mattia De Iulis
SKETCHBOOK

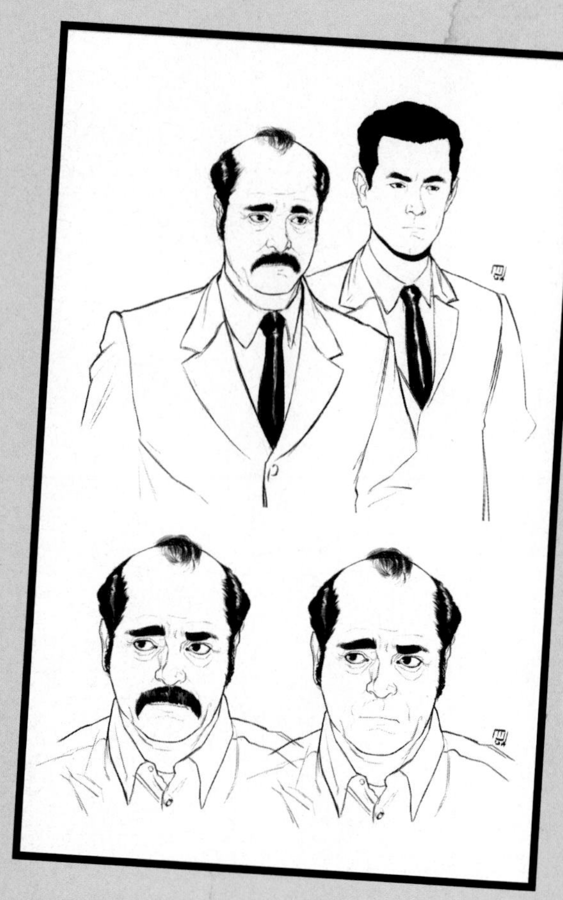